SUCCESS WITH
ACID-LOVING
PLANTS

SUCCESS WITH
ACID-LOVING PLANTS

Graham Clarke

GUILD OF MASTER CRAFTSMAN
PUBLICATIONS LTD

First published 2008 by
Master Craftsman Publications Ltd
astle Place, 166 High Street
wes, East Sussex BN7 1XU

ext © Graham Clarke 2008
the Work GMC Publications Ltd

taken by the author, except for those listed below:

Morguefile.com: front cover; GMC/Eric Sawford: title pages, pages 6, 7, 8, 76–7, 81, 82, 84 (right), 85, 86, 87, 88 (both), 92, 93, 95 (all), 96, 97, 99, 103, 105, 107 (all), 108, 109 (top), 110, 111 (both), 113 (bottom), 114, 115 (both), 117, 119, 121 (both), 122, 123, 124, 125, 126, 127 (all), 128, 129 (top), 131 (both), 132, 133, 134, 135 (bottom), 136, 138 (both), 139, 140 (both), 141, 142, 143, 144 (both), 145, 147 (top left and bottom); GMC/Anthony Bailey: 74 (top right); Scotts MiracleGro: 24 (top right); Mr Fothergills' Seeds: 45 (bottom left and right), 84 (left), 90, Hozelock: 57 (top).

The illustrations on pages 14 and 15 are by Penny Brown.

ISBN-13: 978-1-86108-494-1

A catalogue record for this book is available from the British Library.

Production Manager: Jim Bulley
Managing Editor: Gerrie Purcell
Project Editor: Gill Parris
Managing Art Editor: Gilda Pacitti
Designer: John Hawkins

Set in Futura
Colour origination by GMC Reprographics
Printed and bound in Singapore by Kyodo Printing

Contents

LEFT The archetypal plant for acid soils is the *Rhododendron*, which generally thrives in a woodland situation, on a soil that has been built up with organic matter over many years. This is the cultivar 'Fantastica' AGM.

ABOVE **There are several large plant families that are known for their acid-soil preferences, and these include the** *Magnolia* **genus. This is** *M.* **'Apollo'.**

Introduction

Ask non-gardeners if they live on an acid soil and they will surely think of school lessons in the chemistry laboratory with test tubes of hydrochloric or sulphuric acid. Could the soil actually be made from these? If so, wouldn't it burn you when you touch it? Of course soil can be acidic, as can some fruits and other foodstuffs, including vinegar, or ascetic acid. But the acid content in most soils is only just enough to register in a chemistry test, let alone burn any living thing – animal or vegetable – that happens to come into contact with it.

However, plants react differently in different soils. Over millions of years plants have evolved in shape, size and chemical make-up. They have evolved also in terms of their environmental preferences: some prefer hot, dry places, and others prefer cold, damp places, and others in between.

But some plants have also developed a preference for acidic soils. They prefer their roots to work their way into soil that is strong, fertile and possibly highly organic. These are very often the sorts of plants that grow naturally in dense, woody areas where over many years the soil has been enriched with fallen leaves, which have decayed *in situ* and embellished the soil with their decomposed goodness.

The most common plants that possess these qualities are members of the Ericaceae plant family, which includes heathers, rhododendrons, camellias, as well as a host of other familiar garden plants.

Unfortunately, if you live on a soil that is strongly acidic, the variety of plants you can grow well is limited. Similarly, if you live on a strongly chalky or alkaline soil, there will be a large number of plants that will not thrive. The purpose of this book (and of its companion volume, *Success with Alkaline-Loving Plants*, from the same publisher) is to help those gardeners with one soil or the other. You will be given detail on why your soil is like it is, and how you can create a beautiful garden in spite of it.

Of course, the perfect soil would be fertile and contain plenty of useful and beneficial bacteria. It should not be particularly stony or gravelly, it should be neither pure sand nor heavy clay, and it should not be strongly acid nor alkaline. The perfect soil is neutral – half way between acid and alkaline. Quite a few of us enjoy this status, but millions of us don't, and this is where these books will become very useful.

LEFT **A well-planned and a well-grown planting, such as this mixed border, will only succeed as long as the gardener understands the soil requirements of the plants concerned.**

CHAPTER 1

What is an 'acid' soil?

ABOVE It was during the mid-1800s that scientists first realized that the type of soil you had dictated the kind of plants you could grow. This town garden contains a number of acid-loving plants.

Perhaps a more accurate question to ask would be 'From what is soil made?'. For an acid soil does not contain acid on its own – there are many thousands of components making up the soil, and a few of them are acidic by nature.

As recently as 200 years ago we had little idea what was in our soil but, in the middle of the nineteenth century, scientists analysed plants and found they consisted of at least eight basic elements. The scientists accounted for the carbon, hydrogen and oxygen as coming from the water and the air around us, but that left an array of elements that could only, they deduced, come from the soil. These elements were nitrogen, phosphorous and potassium (the three main ingredients in plant fertilizers, of which much more later), along with calcium and magnesium.

To understand more about what our soil contains, we first need to look at the way in which it was formed.

HOW SOIL DEVELOPED

When a gardener isn't complaining about the weather, it is likely to be about the soil. However, soil is not such a problem as, unlike weather, it can be improved.

The soil is a complex mixture of inert minerals, chemicals and organic materials, and living in amongst all of this is a mass of living organisms from bacteria to fungi, and creatures of sizes from insects, through invertebrates, to mammals.

ABOVE **Soil was formed from the erosion of mountains by the actions of water and ice. Particles settled at the feet of the mountains, and gradually plant life started to inhabit these soil particles. Billions of years later the Earth's natural forestation still exists — in places.**

These organisms digest matter and effectively control the essential processes in the soil that allow plants to grow.

The raw material of a soil is formed from the erosion and weathering of rocks into mixtures of different particle sizes. Over the millennia rocks at the tops of hills, slopes and mountains weathered faster than those at the bases. Through the act of water (and glaciers) and wind, the rock particles were transported to places where they could congregate, and slowly but surely layers of minute rock-soil were formed. In time, as the layers grew deeper they became habitations for the early dry-land plants. And, when these plants died, they formed an organic element to the soils.

After formation the soil was washed by rain containing carbonic acid; this dissolved some of the soil minerals and redistributed them through the soil profile. In doing so, the character of the soil in some places changed. The course of this secondary weathering process is greatly affected by the climate in a given area, and by the type of vegetation covering the soil, so each climatic area in the world tends to produce its own characteristic soil types.

ABOVE **Over millenia, soils have dried in the sun, been transported by glaciers and worn by the wind. Soil particles have settled in places where they gradually build up their layers.**

13

Coarse sand   Fine sand   Silt   Clay

ABOVE **The comparative sizes of different soil particles. A grain of sand is surprisingly large, compared to a particle of clay.**

ABOVE Earthworms are important in that they both help to oxygenate the soil and promote the activity of bacteria, but they often fail to thrive on highly acidic soils.

HOW SOIL BECOMES ACIDIC

The surplus water that drains through a soil gradually removes calcium and other bases (such as the trace elements of magnesium, copper, sulphur, zinc, iron, manganese and molybdenum), and some soils become acidic. This process affects medium and heavy (clay) soils – in which the tiny particles are crowded together in compact masses – less than sandy soils. As a sandy soil becomes acid the plants absorb smaller quantities of base elements (or 'bases'), which include lime. Sandy soils need only lose comparatively small quantities of lime (compared with heavier soils) to become extremely acid, and this loss can occur over a short space of time – even just a few years.

Under very acid soil conditions, plants such as heather and pine become important components of the vegetation. The litter (the dropped foliage and other fading plant matter) from these is mostly deficient in these bases and trace elements, which in time serves to compound the acidity of the soil.

Earthworms, which are so important in good soils because they mix litter with the soil, fail when the soil is particularly acid. As a result, an acid litter layer forms on the soil surface, and as there are hardly any bases or trace elements present, the vegetable acids cannot be neutralized as this litter rots.

These acids are washed downward into the soil by rain. Any bases that are still present are removed, and iron and manganese salts are readily dissolved. This causes the soil to become a greyish colour, which is often mistaken for poor drainage.

CREATION OF 'PANS'

These two particular salts are important because, after they have been carried down through the soil for a short way, they come to a natural level where they remain. They cement together the soil particles in this lower layer, and a hard 'pan' is formed which neither plant roots nor even water can penetrate.

As a result of this process the soil has become not only acid, but also shallow and badly drained, and much of the soil's store of plant nutrients has been lost. A soil of this kind is called a podsol, or 'grey-ash' soil, and is normally formed on sandy areas, particularly where there is heavy rainfall or where the land is covered with pine or heather. Its use to mankind is that the only plants that can possibly grow in it are acid-loving types.

Interestingly, the soil over limestone bedrock can be several feet deep, and in this case the underlying rock will have little or no effect on the soil above it. Rainwater, of course, moves downwards through soil and takes the dissolved

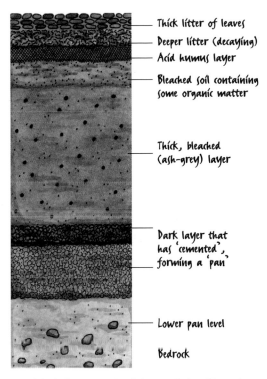

Thick litter of leaves
Deeper litter (decaying)
Acid humus layer
Bleached soil containing some organic matter

Thick, bleached (ash-grey) layer

Dark layer that has 'cemented', forming a 'pan'

Lower pan level

Bedrock

ABOVE A 'podsol', or grey-ash soil, is normally found in sandy areas of high rainfall, or where land is covered in pine or heather.

lime and other bases with it. It is, therefore perfectly feasible for topsoil over a limestone base to become acid.

MEASURING ACIDITY AND ALKALINE CONDITIONS

Essentially, acids are substances capable of releasing hydrogen ions when dissolved in water. Acidity is therefore measured by the concentration of hydrogen ions in water, and is expressed as 'pH', or 'percentage hydrogen'.

The scale is divided from 0 to 14, including decimal placings. The 'neutral' point is pH 7.0. Figures above pH 7.0 indicate alkaline conditions; the higher the figure the more alkaline the conditions. As far as this book is concerned, however, we are more interested in the figures below pH 7.0 which indicate acidity; the lower the figure the stronger the acidity.

The following is a list of specific pH levels that may help in understanding the relevance:

pH 0.1	Hydrochloric acid
pH 0.5	Battery acid
pH 2.6	Strong lemon juice
pH 3.0	Vinegar
pH 4.0 (approx.)	The lower limit for most soils (also beer/coffee)
pH 5.7	Saturated carbonic acid (strong acid rain)
pH 6.5	The ideal pH for soil (i.e. the level that suits the vast majority of plants)
pH 7.0	Neutral point (also human blood/cow's milk)
pH 8.0	Sea water/baking soda
pH 8.5	Upper limit on chalky soil
pH 9.0	Antacid tablets
pH 11.0	Ammonia
pH 12.0	Bleach
pH 12.4	Lime water
pH 13.9	Caustic soda

The pH scale is logarithmic. This means that a change of one pH unit represents a change of x10 in acidity; a change of 2 pH units represents a change of x100 in acidity, and so on. Thus the acidity at pH 4.0 is one thousand times the acidity at pH 7.0.

See page 21, to find out how to determine the pH level of your soil, and what the effects of changing a pH level are.

NATURAL PRODUCTION OF PEAT

One cannot compile a book about acid-loving plants without discussing the subject of peat. But what is it, how is it formed, and why is it relevant to the subject?

In warm, moist, well-aerated soil which has plenty of vegetation, the amount of organic matter can build up each year. And here we have an example of a process that, the more it

ABOVE In some circumstances deposits of vegetable matter can remain wet for long periods, and surface water accumulates in undrained hollows. Under these conditions vegetable matter does not decompose so readily, and over many years will accumulate as peat, and the area becomes a 'peat bog'.

ABOVE **Peat is cut into blocks and is carried away; these blocks are used for fuel in some countries, or taken to a processing plant for bagging for use in the horticultural industry.**

ABOVE **Many gardeners maintain that peat is by far the best of the available 'growing media' but, because it is not sustainable, it is now less used.**

happens the better it works. In other words, the rate of breakdown of the organic matter tends to increase as the organic deposits become greater.

In cool, wet climates the amount of water that falls is very high, and the rate of evaporation is low. Consequently deposits of vegetable matter tend to remain wet for long periods, and surface water accumulates in undrained hollows. Under these conditions vegetable matter does not decompose so readily, and over many years tends to accumulate as peat – which itself is generally of an acidic nature.

On higher land the wet, unrotted peat may form a layer several feet thick, and this is known as 'blanket bog', historically formed mainly from sphagnum moss and deer grass. In poorly drained hollows, vegetable matter accumulates below water level and gradually the deposit fills with water, forming 'basin peat'. The peat is raised above water level by a raised growth of moss.

Peat first became popular with gardeners as recently as the 1950s, when it started to be extracted in quantity. Until this time it was not considered sufficiently high in nutrients for using as a growing medium, and was instead dried and used for fuel. There is some argument, however, over whether peat is renewable or not. Many gardening experts are adamant that it is

and, even more, that its extraction does much to help peoples of some of the poorer nations. There is a massive peat industry, for example, in Lithuania – a country that is ravaged by terrible poverty. Without this industry, the people there will fall into utter destitution. Ironically, the country produces some of the world's finest peat.

I maintain that peat *is* renewable and, if the businesses extracting the peat could finance reinstatement of high water levels in such places, sphagnum mosses will grow again on the cut-away bogs. However, peat cannot be classed as sustainable, as it takes thousands of years to renew.

ABOVE **Bark has become a good and useful alternative to peat; but it must be a fine grade of bark that is specially prepared for potting rather than for use as a mulch or pathway surface.**

MODERN VIEWS ON PEAT AND PEAT ALTERNATIVES

Because of the high use of peat in horticulture, and the increased rate at which it was disappearing from the world's natural peatlands, in 2002 the UK government made a statement saying that it wanted to reduce the use of peat in commercial horticulture, and home gardening, by 90 per cent by 2010. The gardening world – both professional and amateur – is so entrenched in the use of peat, and soil and compost-producing companies are so geared up for the extraction and processing of peat, that this will be difficult to achieve.

Environmentally, most keen gardeners know that peat is a natural product, and we should try to use less of it. But this is where their knowledge stops. But equally, there are many experienced and knowledgeable gardeners who say that peat is by far the best of the available 'growing media' (the term for different composts and soils), and the so-called peat alternatives are just not as good if you want to grow the best flowers, fruits and vegetables.

It is true that when the peat alternatives first came on to the market in the 1990s they gave disappointing results. Flowers were fewer and smaller, and plants appeared to be weaker when compared to other plants growing in peat-based composts. But much work has taken place to improve this, and today the peat alternatives are very much better.

Amateur gardeners use far more peat than professional horticulturists, and there is considerable scope for using more of the alternatives. So, what are they?

ALTERNATIVES TO PEAT

Bark: This comes mainly from renewable conifers and pines, and grades are available from large pieces to fine compost. Some producers claim that bark can act as a complete replacement for peat without any loss of quality.

Woodfibre: This has been used for many years on the Continent, but is relatively new in the UK. It is created from waste wood and is heat- and high-pressure-air treated to open up the fibres and prevent the material from retaining nitrogen. It is used mainly as a bulking agent, added to, reduced-peat composts.

Coir: This is a coarse fibre obtained from the tissues surrounding the seed of the coconut palm. It has several industrial uses (in carpets and brushes) and is increasingly being used as a peat substitute. For composts we extract the cork-like substance, found between the larger fibres, and it is used most successfully in the commercial growing of roses, bulbs and tomatoes.

Green waste: This is the father of them all! Any plant residue can be composted: weeds, grass, dead plants, shredded prunings, vegetable matter – and even sawdust and newsprint. Companies now compost these items, from municipal sources, and convert them into usable, bagged compost. Research has even found that 'green waste' can even contain micro-organisms that inhibit or suppress plant diseases.

This winter, when you're gearing yourself for the coming gardening year, just consider the type of compost you're choosing to use – and make sure it is from a sustainable source.

ABOVE Recycled plant waste on a big scale — companies now specialize in collecting a neighbourhood's plant waste material and composting it on large municipal sites. When properly rotted it is bagged and sold back to gardeners.

ABOVE This cut-away shows a peat bog and how deep these can be — this one is almost 10ft (3m). Some peat is formed in areas where rivers have collected water from chalk hills, so there may be a lime content to the peat.

SOME PEATS CONTAIN LIME

In some of the world's peat reserves, including the Fenlands of Eastern England, the peat was formed in swampy areas where rivers drained through to the open sea. Many of these rivers drain from chalk hills and contain a great deal of dissolved lime. Consequently, peat from these areas is heavily charged with lime and should not be used for acid-loving plants.

Peat containing amounts of lime tends to rot rapidly when it is exposed to oxidation, so deposits can disappear relatively quickly from the landscape.

By contrast acid peat is much more stable, and resistant to decomposition.

CHAPTER 2

Coping with an acid soil

Farmers and professional horticulturists need to know precisely what their soils contain, so they frequently send soil samples away to laboratories for analysis. Such tests will not merely ascertain the pH levels; scientists will look for presence of heavy metal content and chemical residues, and the analysis will also frequently provide a breakdown of soil constituent (sand, clay, silt, loam, and so on).

ABOVE Soils contain many impurities that can inhibit or harm the growth of plants. Professional gardeners therefore send soil samples away for testing. Amateurs can test it themselves.

Amateur gardeners can also send soil away for analysis. However, this is a long, expensive and relatively cumbersome process, and the analysis provided is usually far more detailed than is really necessary for a domestic garden situation. Therefore it is easier and more appropriate for the gardener to test the soil himself or herself.

This is easily done using one of the many amateur soil-testing kits available from garden shops. For just a few pounds you can purchase a pack of small test tubes, with colour charts and a full set of instructions. These kits vary in content and usage according to the make, but they nearly all provide some form of pH analysis, and the more expensive types will also test for presence of nitrogen (seen as N, and needed for all plants but particularly useful for lawns and vegetables), phosphorous (P, particularly useful when growing trees and shrubs) and potash (K, for fruits and flowering plants). The tests are very simple to carry out and take only a few minutes. Some kits also include useful advice about applying fertilizer, how to alter pH and the differing needs of hundreds of plants.

Testing for pH can be carried out at any time of year, but the most accurate readings are usually made in spring or autumn, when the soil is neither too wet nor too dry, and when there is a reasonable temperature without extremes. The following picture panel shows how easy the testing process is.

USING A SOIL-TESTING KIT TO DETERMINE THE pH LEVEL

1 Soil test kits for amateurs are widely available from garden centres.

2 To test for pH levels, carefully open the capsule containing the assessment powder, and put the powder into the test tube.

3 Take a sample of soil from about 4in (10cm) below the surface.

4 Place a small amount of soil into the tube so that it sits on top of the powder.

5 Add water, preferably distilled, according to the instructions.

6 Cap the tube and shake it thoroughly.

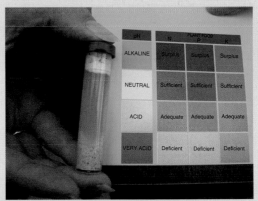

pH	N	PLANT FOOD P	K
ALKALINE	Surplus	Surplus	Surplus
NEUTRAL	Sufficient	Sufficient	Sufficient
ACID	Adequate	Adequate	Adequate
VERY ACID	Deficient	Deficient	Deficient

7 Allow the contents to settle, and compare against the chart. Here you can see that the soil has turned the liquid orange, which clearly indicates that it is classed as acid to very acid.

STRONGLY ACID SOILS MAY CAUSE PROBLEMS

An acid – or sour soil, as it is sometimes called – may be harmful to a plant for three reasons: first, it may reduce the power of the roots to take up some essential plant foods from the soil, such as phosphate; second, it may be short of an essential plant food, and this is usually calcium;

ABOVE and BELOW **Each plant species has a range of pH over which it will grow well, and testing your soil allows you to make a judgement over whether to grow certain plants. Bugle (*Ajuga*) enjoys an acidic soil with pH levels of 4.0–6.0; forget-me-nots (*Myosotis*), however, prefer alkaline soils at pH 6.0–8.0.**

third, it may contain certain metals in an available form that harm the plant, and of these aluminium and manganese are the most important.

ADJUSTING THE pH OF SOIL

Once you have conducted a pH test, you will know whether your soil is alkaline, neutral, acid or very acid, which gives you a general indication of the sorts of plants you can grow with relative ease. Each plant species has a range of pH over which it will grow well; above or below this range it will grow poorly, or fail altogether.

With a slight change in the pH level you may be able to grow a much wider – and therefore rewarding – range of plants.

Raising and lowering pH is not an exact science and most plants have a reasonably wide tolerance, certainly to within 1 pH point. Consult the A–Z section of this book and you will see that the majority can manage well on a pH around 6.5; however, some plants need an alkaline soil and some a particularly acid soil.

Altering pH takes time, so do not expect rapid changes; work steadily towards giving a plant its ideal conditions. Table 1 (on facing page) and Table 2 (on page 24) give approximate amounts to alter pH by 1 pH point up or down the scale, but it is important when you are attempting to alter the pH level of your soil to understand the full range of implications, over and above the acidity rating. For example:

Nutrients: Below pH 5.3 the availability of phosphates falls sharply, and crops are liable to show deficiency. Below pH 5.0 soil may lack bases, such as calcium, potassium and magnesium; acid conditions causes them to be leached easily from the soil.

Trace elements: These are very sensitive to pH changes. At low pH levels they become very soluble, and toxic excesses may occur.

At high pH levels (above 7.5) all the trace elements except one (molybdenum) are much less soluble, and crop deficiencies may occur.

Soil bacteria: Lowering the pH level reduces the activity of nitrifying bacteria and nitrogen fixing bacteria. Below pH 4.5 the activity of soil bacteria ceases.

RAISING THE pH OF VERY ACIDIC SOIL

Carbonic acid in rain leads to a continual loss of lime from the soil; this is worse in some parts of the world than others, depending on the position of industrial areas in relation to the prevailing weather. It means that the soil in such areas is tending to become more acid. In such situations regular applications of lime are necessary, but only sufficient should be applied at any time to raise the pH to 6.5. Less will be needed on sandy than on heavy soils. The effects of acidity on heavy soils are usually less obvious if they do occur, and often no more is produced than a darker brown layer in the subsoil.

Heavier soils naturally carry a cover of broadleaved trees such as beech or oak. Deep roots from these trees absorb calcium and other bases that would otherwise be lost from the soil, and these are returned to the surface of the soil with the leaf litter that falls every autumn. In a beech wood several hundred kilogrammes per hectare (hundredweights per acre) of carbonate of lime are deposited every year in the leaf litter and this prevents the soil from becoming acid.

above In very acidic soils regular applications of lime are necessary, but only sufficient should be applied at any time to raise the pH to 6.5.

The word 'lime' is used so loosely that it no longer has any definite meaning. There are two principal types of liming material commonly available: ground limestone, also called ground chalk or carbonate of lime – $CaCO_3$; hydrated lime, also known as slacked lime or calcium hydroxide – $Ca(OH)_2$. Quicklime, also referred to as burnt lime, or calcium oxide – CaO, can be found but is less common; it should be applied at roughly half the rate of ground limestone.

TABLE 1: To increase soil alkalinity by 1 pH point		
	Addition of ground limestone	Addition of hydrated lime
Sandy soil	6oz per sq yd (203g per m²)	5oz per sq yd (170g per m²)
Loam soil	9oz per sq yd (306g per m²)	7oz per sq yd (240g per m²)
Clay Soil	3oz per sq yd (443g per m²)	9oz per sq yd (306g per m²)

ABOVE If the pH level of soil in a fruit orchard is too high – that is, too alkaline – then grassing down the area and keeping it mown will usually cure the problem.

ABOVE When an acid soil falls below pH 5.3 the availability of phosphates falls sharply. Rectify this by raising the pH level and feeding the area. The expedient way to do this is to apply a general liquid quick-acting fertilizer, modern 'hose-end-dilutors' are available to assist in supplying fertilizer across a large area.

LOWERING THE pH OF VERY ALKALINE SOIL

The level of soil pH can be reduced by the addition of acid materials (see Table 2, below). If flowers of sulphur is added to soil it is slowly converted to sulphuric acid by soil bacteria. It is often added to soils rich in lime to make it possible to grow such plants as rhododendrons and heathers.

Ammonia-containing fertilizers, and in particular sulphate of ammonia, will remove lime from soil and lower soil pH.

Acid peat may be dug into the soil. This can work extremely well (provided that there is no large reserve of available calcium carbonate in the soil). In general it has little effect on heavy soils with a large lime reserve.

TABLE 2: To increase soil acidity by 1 pH point (all soils):

	Add
Sulphate of ammonia	2oz per sq yd (70g per m^2)
Flowers of sulphur	2oz per sq yd (70g per m^2)
Peat	44oz per sq yd (1.5kg per m^2)
Compost heap	272oz per sq yd (9.25kg per m^2)
Manure	88oz per sq yd (3kg per m^2)

The pH of sandy soils may be lowered fairly easily (just as it may be easily raised with a small dressing of lime), compared with a heavy soil. It is therefore much easier to over-lime and under-lime sandy soils than heavy soils.

Many plants – essentially the acid-lovers – will not grow in calcareous or alkaline soils, particularly if the level is approaching pH8 or higher. Plants may show chlorotic leaves, a condition known as lime-induced chlorosis. It can be cured to some extent by lowering the pH of the soil a little, or by dressings of organic manures or composts, or by the use of substances known as iron chelates. If it occurs in an apple orchard, grassing down the orchard and keeping the grass mown will usually cure the trouble. It is, however, important when you are attempting to alter the pH level of your soil to understand the full range of implications, so refer to my comments on pages 22–23.

ABOVE **Animal manure (this is horse) is the best bulky material for adding to the soil.**

THE IMPORTANCE OF HUMUS

The most fertile soils are slightly acid; extremely acid soils will grow little but moss and sedge. On a soil in the range of pH 5.0–6.5, the gardener is fortunate since, with certain reservations, many things will grow in it. One of the reservations may be that the soil is lacking in humus. This is rotted organic matter that bulks out the soil, improving its structure and moisture retention.

If the natural soil is deficient in humus it must be made good by the addition of suitable materials. This is relevant to all soils, but particularly so in the case of a sandy one. Without adding humus to a barren soil one's efforts would lead to poor results.

If you are growing vegetables, whatever type of soil you have you should dig it over once a year and, whenever possible, incorporate plenty of humus – in other words compost or farmyard manure (if you can get hold of it).

Manure is the best material if you want to feed the soil and increase its moisture-retaining capabilities; manure from pigs and horses is most commonly available, usually from farms that put up signs. Sometimes a town-based garden centre will be able to order it in for you. It is not particularly expensive, but it is heavy and doesn't prevent weed growth – it does, however, produce luxuriant plant growth. Poultry manure is also available, but is very strong and needs to dry out for use as a fertilizer dressing rather than manure. Do remember that the compost or manure has to be well rotted before use as, if it rots while it is in the ground, it can deplete the soil in the immediate vicinity of much-needed nitrogen.

Work the bulky matter, which improves the soil texture and fertility, into the soil at the time of digging. The addition of such material is recommended for many soil types, including clay, where it helps to open up the sticky soil, so improving the drainage of rainwater. Conversely, organic matter also helps free-draining soils such as sands and gravels, to hold on to moisture and plant foods, since it acts like a sponge.

The organic matter is added to the trenches while digging, at a rate of at least one level barrowload per 4sq yd (3.7m²). Digging should be carried out regularly on the vegetable plot and beds used for bedding plants, generally in autumn, and it should always be carried out prior to planting permanent plants (trees, shrubs, perennials, and so on) and even before laying a lawn.

Apart from manure and home-made compost the peat alternatives described on page 18 are also relevant for digging in – but unlike both manure and home compost, they are not generally rich in nutrient value, their main benefits being in terms of improving the soil's structure.

IMPROVING DRAINAGE ON A HEAVY SOIL

A clay soil during a wet winter can be a miserable quagmire, and in the heat of the summer it can bake hard like concrete. Neither condition is appropriate to good plant growth, so you should do something about it. Certainly adding one of the bulky organic matters discussed above will do wonders, particularly over a period of time. However, there are three 'inorganic' types of improver that, in their own way, are just as important, depending on the pH level of your soil. So, before applying these you should conduct a soil test so that you can decide whether you want to apply them.

Gypsum This is sulphate of lime, and is used on clay soils to improve texture and workability, and to reduce stickiness. Unlike lime, however, gypsum does not increase alkalinity in the soil so can safely be used on acid soils that you wish to remain acidic. It is also ideal for alkaline soils, as they won't be made more alkaline. Sprinkle it onto dug ground during autumn and allow it to lie over winter, then fork it in. Apply at the rate of 8oz per sq yd (226g per m²).

Lime This is only useful for adding to sticky clay soils if you are happy for the pH level to change. Lime improves the soil texture and makes it easier to cultivate. Apply it in the same way as gypsum, but if manure has been applied during the digging, wait a few months before applying the lime, as the two substances can react badly with each other. Lime should be applied to a clay soil once every five years, but to a sandy soil every two or three years is sufficient, as the lime will be washed out by rain.

An alternative to lime, but with a similar effect, is calcified seaweed. Like a type of coral, it can be bought in packs, and contains a number of minor plant foods. It is more expensive, however.

Coarse sand or grit A 2in (5cm) deep layer of this, dug in 8in (20cm) below the surface of clay soil, will open up the soil, allowing rainwater to drain through more easily and swiftly.

ABOVE **Coarse sand, along with grit, is available from builders' merchants, and can be used to improve drainage on a heavy, or clay, soil.**

ABOVE **Home-made compost provides valuable humus to hungry soils.**

MAKING HOME COMPOST

One thing I am very keen to promote with all gardeners is the art of making their own compost; modern parlance refers to it as 'recycling garden waste'.

How is compost made? Essentially it is just old plants, or bits of old plants, that are allowed to rot down.

Annual plants come to the end of their lives every autumn; biennials at the end of their second year; perennials after a number of years when they've become too old or we've become fed up with them and dug them up. And then, of course, there are weeds: these tend to die whenever I can get hold of them! All of these things can be put on to a compost heap.

Other things to add to a compost heap include peelings and unused bits of vegetables from the kitchen, as well as grass mowings, shredded prunings and any other bits of soft, green matter.

Even small amounts of paper, if shredded by an office shredder, can be added. All of these items will rot down to a fraction of their former size, and in so doing will become good, available humus enabling other plants to grow.

Prunings from woody shrubs and trees do need to be shredded: wood tends to take forever to rot.

ABOVE **Peelings and unused bits of vegetables — and old tea bags — can be added to the compost heap.**

ABOVE **If you are adding woody items such as conifer and hedge clippings to the compost heap, make sure they are shredded into small pieces.**

ABOVE **Making good home-grown compost can take as long as a year, or as little as six weeks (in the summer).**

There are some things that should not go on to a compost heap:

- General household rubbish of plastics, metals and glass.
- Roots of perennial weeds such as couch grass, ground elder, bindweed, docks and dandelions, as these will almost certainly continue to grow and you'll end up spreading them around the garden.
- Cooked food – such as meat, fish, cheese and grease. Aside from smelling bad (rotting meat and dairy food smells completely different to rotting raw vegetable matter), you could be encouraging rats and other unwanted visitors.

However, the smaller the prunings, the quicker they'll decompose. In essence, soft things are best for a compost heap, so the rule is: the harder the material, the smaller it should be.

Do not put too much of any single substance on to a compost heap, as the secret to making good compost is the 'little-and-often' principle. You should aim for a really good mixture of materials.

As for the structure of the heap, take a trip to the garden centre and you'll discover a range of enclosed bins to keep the area neat and tidy. If you prefer, you could simply knock together four upright posts and encircle them with chicken wire. The edges will become dry and will take longer to rot, but inside the heap things should rot down perfectly well.

Making good compost can take as little as six weeks, if it is the height of summer and you add just small bits of green matter and some activator – usually a nitrogen-based substance that speeds up the rotting process. Or it can take a year or more, if there are lots of thick, dry autumn leaves, or a fair amount of shredded wood, or you started the heap in the autumn (the speed of rotting decreases in winter).

The end result will be a wonderful, friable, dark, fine material that can be dug into the soil as described above. If it is fine enough, it could even be used as a seed compost. Or it can be used as a mulch (see facing page).

Finally, garden recycling of leaves – that is, the art of making leafmould – is entirely relevant in a garden with acid soil. Leafmould is made by laying down rotted leaves, collected together and compressed over several years. It adds fibre to the soil, improves drainage and helps to retain moisture. It is also the perfect conditioner for an acid soil, as it enhances the acidity without increasing the pH level. You can rarely find leafmould to buy, however, which means making your own is the only real practical option – if you have access to many broad-leaved trees.

WHAT IS 'MULCHING'?

A mulch is a layer of organic (or inorganic) material applied around plants and on top of the soil surface. For several reasons it is beneficial to spread a 2in (5cm) layer of mulch over a warmed, moist soil in spring: this prevents evaporation of soil moisture; suppresses weed growth (if weeds do seed in the mulch they are easily pulled up); and, finally, the mulch will gradually add to the humus content of the soil through the action of earthworms.

Home-made composts and leafmould are full of plant goodness and are the first choice for anyone who wants to maintain a good quality acidic soil. Farmyard manure is also excellent, but a ready supply is not so easily sourced.

Again, these materials should be applied when they are well rotted. If applied in a raw state, their composite strength (acidic and high in ammonia) could damage the soil or any live plant material it touches. In fact, even in its well-rotted state, it should not be laid so that it touches the plants, as it will cause 'burning'.

ABOVE **Putting down organic mulch, here around roses, suppresses weeds, helps retain soil moisture and aids soil nutrition.**

ABOVE **Cocoa shell mulch is becoming increasingly popular – and it can even make the border smell of chocolate for a while!**

ABOVE **Fabric mulches, although not particularly good to look at, do prevent weed growth and reduce soil evaporation.**

TWO LESS-COMMON MULCHING MATERIALS

Straw: This can be used to great effect on an allotment, but in a garden setting it could be considered unsightly. Weed seeds may come with the straw, so defeating one of the objects of putting down a mulch. Apply a nitrogen-based fertilizer to the area, to replenish the loss of nitrogen from the soil caused by the decomposition of the straw.

Grass clippings: Short clippings from the lawn can be used as a shallow mulch – but keep them away from the crowns of the plants as they could 'suffocate' the breathing pores of the plants, especially when they start to rot down. The clippings mulch may be topped up as required. Do not use a mulch of this if your lawn is weedy.

ABOVE After a few weeks the colour of the cocoa shell mulch fades and more closely matches the natural soil colour.

Bark is relatively cheap, light, and bio-degradable and has excellent moisture-retaining and weed-suppressing qualities. It is available in colours other than 'natural'.

In commercial landscaping bark in green, gold and black chips is highly popular, but for domestic gardens the tendency is usually to go for something more natural in colour. The disadvantage to using bark is that it needs topping up most years, and its appearance is not to everyone's taste. It is, however, an excellent surface for pathways, and is safe where children are running about.

Cocoa bean shells, coir fibre and even hair mulches are available. There are also a number of different fabric mulches for allowing rain through, whilst preventing (or at least reducing) water evaporation from the soil.

ABOVE Shredded bark is relatively cheap, light and biodegradable, and makes a good mulching material or surface for pathways.

ABOVE **A thin layer of gravel will afford some moisture retention in the soil, but lay a weed-preventing fabric under it first.**

ABOVE **Glass nuggets are used sometimes, particularly in contemporary garden designs, as a decorative mulch.**

DECORATIVE MULCHING

Many alpines and rock plants are happiest when a layer of stone chippings or small-grade gravel is laid around them, as these stop water and mud splashing up on to the leaves. Stone mulches are long-lasting and there is a huge range of colours and size grades to choose from. A disadvantage is that in the autumn, when leaves fall, it is difficult to sweep or clear the area.

A thin layer of gravel will afford some moisture retention in the soil but, to be effective, the layer should be 3in (7.5cm) thick, or more. However thick a gravel mulch, weeds always seem to germinate in it, but they are usually quite easy to remove. It is important to lay down a weed-preventing membrane (available from garden centres) before putting down the chips. A popular alternative to natural yellowish or brown gravel is chipped slate, in shades of plum, blue, or grey.

Finally, glass nuggets can be used as a decorative mulching material. They are safe, as the sharp edges have been rounded off during manufacture but, although it has similar qualities to gravel, it is much more expensive and does not always blend well with the planting schemes in traditional gardens. In spite of this, glass nuggets are available in a range of bright colours, and modern garden designers use them extensively in their contemporary schemes.

CHAPTER 3

How to design a garden on acid soil

ABOVE An acid soil need not comprise just heathers and rhododendrons. There is wide range of acid-loving plants, with a multitude of different forms, shapes and sizes.

I mentioned in Chapter 1 that some conifers (mainly pines) and members of the heather plant family (Ericaceae), were natural inhabitants of areas on acid soil. But there is much more to the world of 'gardening on acid' than this.

Essentially, creating a garden on an acid soil is no different from creating one on chalk, clay, silt or sand. It is simply a matter of choosing the right plants, and incorporating them in such a way that they develop in the optimum way and in the most attractive way.

FRESH GARDEN, FRESH START

If you are fortunate enough to move to a garden on acid soil that is bare – perhaps left fresh after the builders have gone, or the garden is just laid down to grass – then you will have a wealth of design possibilities before you.

The first task should be to commit the garden to paper. If you are planning beds, borders, lawn, patio/deck, and possibly things like a pond or shed, then it is best if you produce a scale drawing or plan of the area. This must include all of the garden's 'fixtures and fittings', i.e. the house, greenhouse/conservatory, immovable and desirable trees and shrubs, the driveway, paving and walling, drains, sewers and sumps, electricity poles, and so on. The best way to start a paper plan is to conduct your own 'survey' of the garden.

Walk around the house (and any fixed outbuildings) and make a large sketch of the layout, in plan form but not necessarily to scale. A long, flexible measuring tape is useful, and a good starting point is a particular part of the house, say the back door.

Mark on the plan the ideal places for the most important elements of your future garden (patio, lawn, greenhouse, vegetable garden, and so on as appropriate). The remaining places will be left for you to put in your favourite acid loving plants. The designs of the beds and borders that contain these plants will be dependant on the types of plants they are.

ABOVE In terms of garden design, the very best start is the 'blank canvas': a garden that is entirely bare, perhaps left fresh after the builders have gone, or laid down to grass.

ABOVE Before you undertake any construction work you should commit your plan to paper — and then live with this for a few days to make sure you like the planned changes.

ABOVE Clearly mark on your paper plan the position of garden fixtures, such as greenhouses…

ABOVE … and hedges. Both of these will inevitably prove time-consuming or difficult to remove or re-site.

HEATHER AND CONIFER GARDENS

Heathers are delightful, tough little plants, although they are not particularly in fashion at the moment, which is a shame. They deserve to be grown more.

Most members of the heather family – which includes rhododendrons, azaleas, camellias, pieris, pernettyas, gaultherias and a host of other familiar shrubby plants – require an acid soil. These plants would not necessarily die if grown in a neutral or chalky soil, but most would not like it and their garden performance would be sadly lacking.

There are few plants that have had such a chequered history over the past 150 years as heathers. During the Victorian period, and the first part of the twentieth century, they were planted as flowers at the front of beds and borders.

Then they went out of vogue. It wasn't until the 1970s that they were put on the map again, and were sold in their tens of millions, and it is largely down to one man.

A nurseryman in Norfolk, England, by the name of Adrian Bloom realized that heathers went very well with garden and dwarf conifers, and came up with some different planting schemes. Famously he transformed somebody's front garden on a television programme, planting it exclusively with heathers and conifers, and it caused a sensation. All of a sudden heathers were thrust in front of us, and garden centres ran out of stock very quickly. In the 1990s their popularity started to decline once again, and today there are many fewer commercial producers of heathers than there were even five years ago.

ABOVE **Heather gardens, which also included a few conifers because of the similarity of their fine, close-knit foliage, became very popular in the 1970s.**

So, how can we encourage more gardeners to grow heathers? Well, to start with, pests and diseases hardly ever affect them. Second, there are different types flowering at different times, and you can have heathers blooming in your garden near enough all year long. Third, when honeybees are active, the heather flowers are very popular. I'm not an expert on honey, but I'm told that heather honey has a very distinctive and desirable taste.

Conifers usually take an important but secondary role in such planting schemes. They look good with the heathers as the foliage is similarly small, but the extra height that conifers provide gives a heather bed another dimension. Do not plant the heathers too close to the conifers; some forms of heather, including cultivars of *Erica carnea* such as 'Pink Spangles'

and 'Springwood White' can climb up into the conifers and other nearby plants. Sometimes this can cause the bases of the conifers to go bare, which becomes all too visible if you ever want to dig up the heather or move the conifer.

Mixing colours is a personal choice. The intense crimson and deep golden hues of some frosted winter-flowering heathers can be very eye-catching, and carpets of golden heathers will set off blue or green conifers. However, it is best to widen the palette to include other plants to add variety of texture, shape, size and colour.

You need not, of course restrict yourself to heathers and conifers in your heather and conifer garden – bulbs, perennials and small shrubs can all be used to great effect. Ornamental grasses can be particularly striking in such a bed.

ABOVE **Height to an essentially low heather garden can be provided by taller conifers and, as seen here, a well-placed raised bed.**

ABOVE **Heathers can also be used to great effect on a rock garden – with pockets of acid soil between the rock layers.**

RHODODENDRON AND WOODLAND GARDENS

Rhododendrons will thrive on acid soil. There is a terrific range of varieties available, so it is possible to have varieties in flower from late winter to mid-summer. But selecting the right ones needs care, as many grow far too large for a small or medium-sized garden. Fortunately there are many excellent smaller varieties, and a good number of dwarf species and hybrids.

It is not a good idea to rely solely on rhododendrons for your garden colour as they have a distinct flowering period, but for the remainder of the year they comprise basic garden greenery. They are, of course, woodland plants, and for this reason they look best when planted as part of – or to create – a woodland situation within the garden. They do not generally mind being in the shade of taller trees; in fact, rhododendrons (and azaleas, and the closely related camellias and pieris) actually suffer if planted in full sun. During summer when the sun is at its hottest and strongest these woodland plants can overheat, dehydrate, and the foliage can turn yellow. Hydrangeas and other acid-tolerant shrubs combine well with them, as do heathers and certain grasses, and such companions will usefully extend the season of interest.

ABOVE **Some rhododendrons can become huge affairs, with the dimensions of medium-sized trees.**

ABOVE **After heathers, rhododendrons are the most famous of acid-loving plants; they are best suited to woodland situations.**

PEAT GARDENS AND BEDS

Peat looks, feels and is the stuff that plant roots like best to burrow in, even though peat itself does not have great food value for plants. It actually has very little. Its virtue lies in its texture and its ability to absorb and retain vast amounts of moisture.

Peat gardens were conceived as ways of cultivating and cosseting small plants that, usually, prefer damp acid soil and a moist atmosphere (as found in woodlands and misty moorlands). Such plants are found almost everywhere in the world's rainy highlands. Many of them are alpines in the strict sense, but not rock plants: their only interest in a rock would be to hide in its shade. The peat garden is therefore complementary to the rock garden. However, the peat garden is far easier, quicker and cheaper to build than a rock garden, and the range of plants that can be grown in peat (if conditions are slightly modified, such as adding more stones for drainage, or lime) is huge.

A peat garden is a bed of acid soil richly and deeply laced with peat, in a proportion of about half and half, sloping preferably away from the sun (that means towards the north if you live in the northern hemisphere, and towards the south if you live in the southern hemisphere).

ABOVE **Peat gardens can make a perfect home for Japanese azaleas, close members of the *Rhododendron* family.**

A sunless slope, or the shady side of a wall, can thus be converted from a problem corner to one where a wide range of plants can thrive.

Peat gardens should also be well supplied with rain or other soft water, but also adequately drained, with rubble below if necessary. The softness of the water is crucial – water from a chalk spring would be useless.

When peat gardens first became popular in the middle of the last century, the beds were usually sloped, and edged with low walls ideally built of solid blocks of peat. In Europe such brick-sized blocks were (and are still) cut from peat beds. Plants set their roots – and seed – into these blocks, covering them with a mantle of vegetation and at the same time binding the structure together.

These days, owing to the concerns over depletion of the world's natural peat stocks (see Chapter 1) it is considered politically incorrect for such a large volume of peat to be used simply for decorating someone's garden. Modern convention has it that educational establishments, such as botanic gardens, can legitimately use peat blocks in this way, but domestic gardeners should find an alternative solution (see Chapter 1, page 18. 'Modern views on peat and peat alternatives').

CONTAINER GARDENS

The beauty of using containers in your acid-soil garden – whether troughs, pots, tubs, urns, vases, hanging baskets, windowboxes and even growing bags – is that, by choosing compost mixtures with a higher pH, you will be able to grow some alkaline-loving plants, which widens your choice.

Likewise, of course, if you have a largely alkaline soil, you can grow acid-loving plants in containers.

BUILDING A PEAT GARDEN

ABOVE **If your acid or peat bed is too large to reach across, to avoid compacting the soil set some small stepping stones down.**

For peat gardens the rules are simple. Do not attempt to install one in an area of very alkaline soil or water supply, or very low rainfall. It will be a great deal of trouble and probably only moderately successful.

Make sure that these gardens are weeded thoroughly at the time of construction, and regularly thereafter. Weeds with running roots will absolutely adore this kind of situation.

After your chosen area has been weeded, either use peat block or, more appropriately, log edging. Logs of wood are, in a purist sense, not as good as peat blocks as plants will not root into them as vigorously as they do the peat. However, there are certain benefits to using wood edging: the first is that it is easier to get hold of these days; the second is that it makes a very definite edging, whereas the peat blocks in time collapse and look a bit like an undulating border; the third is that it is better for the environment.

ABOVE Containers are very popular in gardens that are strongly acid – or strongly alkaline – as they enable you to grow plants with the opposite soil. Here there is a mixture of summer-flowering marguerites, conifers and acers

However, if you do decide to use peat blocks, make sure that they are damp as, once dry, all peat is extremely hard to re-wet. For the same reason each block should be partly buried in the soil so that it constantly absorbs moisture, and doesn't dry out.

Build walls with a backward tilt into the slope. Old gardeners used to nail the blocks together with thick wire. Fill the void behind the blocks, and between them where required, with a peat-and-soil mixture. Embrace, if possible, the shade from big trees but do not build directly under one; its autumn leaves and constant year-round drips from the rain can cause problems.

If the peat bed (or 'acid bed') is too large to reach across, set down some small stepping stones; these will help by concentrating any compacted areas and will make working in wet conditions a little less muddy.

ABOVE Wooden logs make an acceptable edging to a peat bed, but the best type of edging is that of peat blocks, although because of concerns of depletion of natural peat reserves these are not as politically acceptable these days.

ABOVE **Variegated hostas, with their large billowing leaves, make excellent container plants – but watch out for slugs.**

ABOVE **A group of containerized ornamental grasses can look most effective grouped together on a patio or deck.**

Ornamental plants The most suitable types of container for permanent acid-loving plants are pots, tubs, urns and vases; there is a wide range of these on the market, and they can be made from wood, plastic, terracotta, reconstituted stone and moulded resin. The plastic ones are the cheapest, but look for those that are not too obtrusive. The most popular colours for plastic are white, green and brown.

These containers are best used for seasonal displays of annuals (mainly bedding plants) and bulbs. When in full flowering glory, they make very effective focal points. They are, of course, ideal for standing on a patio, path, driveway, or next to a door. But they can also look very good when stood in borders. The tubs, raised slightly on blocks, can be placed in a part of the garden that is not at its best when the plants in the tub are at their prettiest.

The first thing to do when planting your tub is to get it in its final position before you start (it will be heavy to move when full). If it's for summer, put a tray underneath to help make a water reservoir. Now put into the base some coarse material, such as broken flower pots, pea gravel or washed stones. Do not completely block the drainage hole in the bottom of the pot (and if there are no drainage holes, then you should drill some), but you do need to allow excess water to be able to escape.

Then fill the tub two thirds full, and firm the compost as you go. Use a soil- or loam-based compost. An acid peat-based compost (or a coir alternative) will do quite well, but drying out in summer can be more of a problem. If compost is allowed to dry out, the plants will not be able to suck up what they need to survive (let alone thrive). So it is a good idea to mix water-retaining polymer granules that are widely available into the compost as you plant (some composts now include granules as standard). The polymers absorb moisture from the compost when it is watered or rained upon, and then release this moisture to thirsty plant roots when the compost dries out.

ABOVE **If your garden has alkaline soil one of the best ways to grow blue hydrangeas is to grow them in containers.**

ABOVE **A wide range of fruits and vegetables can be grown in pots, but you will need to watch the watering and feeding.**

The best plants to put into a tub already come in pots. Remove the pots and set the plants in the tub where they are to go. As a guide, one plant in the centre and four or five around the edge of tub 12in (30cm) across is about right. Set each plant so that the surface of its root ball is 1in (2.5cm) below the rim of the tub. Fill around the root balls with more compost, firm gently and water well.

Permanent plants, such as small trees (dwarf fruit trees can be very successful), conifers, flowering shrubs and even some perennials (such as forms of *Hosta*) can look fabulous in containers – although they do not necessarily have the long summer of vibrant colour that you can get with annuals. The beauty of growing acid-loving plants in a large tub is that you can provide them with one of the ericaceous composts

widely available from garden centres, and they will they grow happily, whatever the status of your main garden soil.

Fruit and vegetables The range of food crops that can be grown in containers is wide, but some are easier to grow than others.

If you have little available space for growing fruit trees, some smaller types can be grown in large tubs.

There are two important provisos, however: first, you should use as large a container as possible and, second, you should only grow a tree that has been grown on a 'dwarfing rootstock'. This means that the variety has been grafted on to special roots, which keep it dwarf (these trees are also often earlier fruiting).

41

Strawberries are ideal container plants, and special strawberry barrels are available. These cylindrical plastic barrels are filled with compost and strawberry plants are set through holes in the sides and the top. I have even seen barrels on bases that rotate, so all plants can get some direct sunshine. Also, some barrels have a central tube for watering, and this is very useful as it helps ensure that water reaches the bottom of the barrel – this is hard to achieve in a well-filled barrel that you water from the top, as plants in the top half soak up the water before it can reach the plants lower down.

Some herbs – such as parsley, tarragon, chives, rosemary, thyme and mint – do well in containers, too. In fact, I only ever grow mint (*Mentha*) in containers, as all forms are vigorously invasive and will grow into other nearby plants. Growing them in a container keeps them under control. Mint is also an alkaline-loving plant, so if you have an acid garden soil it is unlikely to be very successful, unless it is grown in pots.

RAISED BEDS

In reality these garden features are no more than large, permanently sited containers. They can be made of ornamental stone, concrete blocks, bricks, or even old railway sleepers (available from specialist suppliers, usually listed in your local telephone directory).

The side wall of a raised bed, unlike a tall brick wall or the side of a building, does not usually need footings, or a foundation. However, these structures do retain an often heavy bank of soil, and you do not want them to collapse under the pressure. When I have constructed these in the past I have dug a trench – some 4in (10cm) deep – along the line of where the wall will be, and into this trench I have poured bags of a cement-concrete ready-mix.

Smooth the surface and then water it lightly with a rosed watering can, and leave it overnight. The next day you will have a sturdy base, bonded to the surrounding soil and on to which you can build your retaining wall.

ABOVE **Raised beds are really just large, permanently sited containers. But the bigger they are the more you can do with them. This modern white-sided bed is filled with bright summer-flowering begonias and lilies.**

With this kind of footing, however, the wall should be no more than four courses high.

The area within the raised bed should be dug over, and any weeds removed. Add well-rotted manure or compost as you go. When I had a garden that was on an alkaline soil I wanted to create a raised acid bed and as there was no soil available from anywhere else within the garden I bought topsoil to fill the bed. I added to the topsoil several bags of peat and ericaceous compost, and I then had a bed suitable for acid-lovers.

If you wish to grow mainly alpine plants in your raised bed, good drainage becomes more of an issue, and you should add an extra part of coarse sand.

Once the bed has been dug, weeded and filled with the appropriate soils and/or compost, water it well. Leave it for a day or two to settle and then you can begin to plant.

ABOVE This raised bed was constructed in one of the author's previous gardens. It was designed to be an acid bed in a largely alkaline garden.

The taller plants should be towards the centre of the bed, with the shorter ones at the front and do not, of course, forget to grow a few trailing kinds to hang down the sides.

ABOVE A more traditional brick-sided raised bed is appropriate to a more traditional or cottage garden situation.

CHAPTER 4

Buying, planting and growing acid-loving plants

ABOVE **When buying plants there is only one simple rule: always buy the best quality and most expensive plants you can afford. Choosing cheap plants is usually false economy.**

Once you have identified your soil type, and you have understood the parameters between which you can grow acid-loving plants successfully, and you have decided where you want to grow them, you will need to go out and buy them. The choice of plants is, frankly, enormous, and the different ways to buy and set them out can bewilder a beginner to gardening – and sometimes the more experienced of us as well. Let's look at the key plant groups.

ANNUALS, BIENNIALS AND BEDDING PLANTS

Annuals are plants that are sown, grow, flower and die all within a year, whereas biennials are sown and grown on in one year, and flower and die during a second year. 'Bedding plants' is the term used to describe plants of either type, which are generally grown in quantity, and planted in 'beds', for a massed display.

Familiar annuals with a preference for acid soils include snapdragon (*Antirrhinum*), pot marigold (*Calendula*), sunflower (*Helianthus*), flowering tobacco (*Nicotiana*) and busy lizzie (*Impatiens*).

Bedding plants are usually sold in trays or pots and, depending on the type, are available from six months before they are due to flower, right up until they have already started to flower.

Buying When choosing any plants, look for healthy specimens. There should be no weeds, or pests or diseases present, and the plants should not yet have started flowering, so that you have a full season of colour ahead of you. If they have already started blooming, the plants will have developed a significant root system and may respond badly when planted out, and you will also have missed some of the flowering potential. If the plants you desire have all started to flower whilst still on the shop's shelves, go for the trays, or plants, with the fewest flowers.

Planting Most annual types will be tender, so will be damaged by frost or very cold weather. They will have been started off in a greenhouse, so will need very slow acclimatization in spring to colder conditions – a process known as 'hardening off'. They should not, of course, be fully planted out in the garden or in containers until all danger of frosts has passed.

ABOVE Annuals and bedding plants are usually grown for bright, massed displays of summer colour.

ABOVE Antirrhinums, or snapdragons, are acid-loving plants and best treated as annuals; they provide long-lasting bright colour throughout summer.

ABOVE Calendulas, or pot marigolds, are hardy annuals, often sown in the autumn of one year, for flowering during summer and early autumn of the next.

45

ABOVE Bedding plants are generally sold in trays from the garden centre. Do not buy plants that are already in flower as you will have missed much of their total flowering potential.

Before planting, fork the soil over, making sure that any annual weeds are completely buried. Perennial weeds, however, should be removed as these will re-grow if left. To feed the bedding plants through the season, apply a sprinkling of general fertilizer evenly over the soil, following the manufacturer's instructions.

Give the plants a thorough watering an hour or two before planting them, so that they are not stressed prior to the move. If the bedding plants are in individual pots, take them out gently and place them in a hole dug with a trowel. The hole should be the same size as the pot. Firm them in place with your hands and water them in.

Most young bedding plants these days come in plastic or polystyrene strips; you will need to either break the strips apart, or gently tease the plants out of their compartments. Transplant them carefully: damaged leaves will readily be replaced with new leaves, within reason, but a plant only has one stem so avoid causing it harm.

ABOVE When planting bedding plants make sure they are spaced out well (giving sufficient room to develop) and firmed in position well, but not so much that you damage the roots.

ABOVE After firming, water the plants in. This should be done as quickly as possible, as the plant roots that were exposed during the planting process could dry out and quickly perish.

BULBS

The most often seen bulbs are the spring-flowerers, including daffodils (*Narcissus*), tulips, crocuses, hyacinths, and so on. Daffodils, particularly, prefer acid conditions. The earlier-flowering bulbs, appearing in winter and into early spring, include snowdrops (*Galanthus*) and winter aconites (*Eranthis*). In summer there are lilies, *Gladiolus* and dahlias and lily-of-the-valley (*Convallaria*); this last bulb enjoys a wide pH range with soil, even as low as pH4.5. In the autumn there are bold forms of *Colchicum*, *Sternbergia* and *Schizostylis*. Of these, the colchicums are the most tolerant of acid soil.

Buying The first of the new season's mail order bulb catalogues are sent out to customers in mid-summer, and ordering early has many advantages: those that require early planting, such as colchicums and daffodils, will be with you in good time; also, if you delay ordering, some varieties may be sold out later in the season. The range of bulbs available by mail order is extensive and includes unusual varieties, but do not be afraid to complain or send the bulbs back if they turn out to be below standard.

In garden centres bulbs will also be on display from mid-summer onwards, offering the opportunity to browse, choose and plan your

The following important points should be remembered when selecting bulbs from a shop:

- Avoid any bulbs that do not have a clean base, that are soft and show signs of rot, or that have started to shoot, producing more than a very small amount of growth.
- Select plump, firm, and well-rounded examples. Lily bulbs should be fleshy and firm, and avoid any that are dried out. Larger bulbs usually result in the finest flower spikes.

In the spring many summer-flowering bulbs and tubers will be on sale, the same rules of buying apply. Store bulbs in a cool, dry place, never near heaters — and never in plastic bags as this makes them sweat. Open any bags before planting to let air circulate.

display. There is much useful information on colour, height and growing to be found on accompanying point-of-sale material.

Planting Plant out bulbs out as soon as possible; label the place to avoid any accidental damage. Textbooks often quote very specific depths for bulbs when they are planted.

ABOVE An area of 'naturalized' daffodils (that is, growing in grass and looking natural) is one of the joys of a spring garden.

ABOVE During autumn — the main season for buying and planting spring-flowering bulbs — garden centres open up large 'bins' from where the customers can pick and choose their own bulbs.

ABOVE *Colchicum speciosum* 'Atrorubens' is a most colourful autumn-flowering bulb for the acid-soil garden. Sometimes called 'naked ladies', as its flowers appear before any of the leaves.

ABOVE Some people like to interplant bulbs and other spring-bedding plants. Here, a crown imperial (*Fritillaria imperialis*) is being planted between wallflowers.

ABOVE The most natural-looking woodland garden on acid soil must have a carpet of snowdrops, forms of *Galanthus*.

As a general rule, however, a bulb should be planted so that there is as much soil above it as the height of the bulb itself – you won't go far wrong with this. Exceptions are bluebells and daffodils, which should be planted twice their own depth.

The spring-flowering bulbs are the first to be planted during the 'bulb year' and these should go in during the autumn.

Daffodils and other forms of *Narcissus* could be planted in late summer or beginning of autumn, as they produce roots early.

The majority of bulbs, with the exception of tulips, can be planted as soon as the summer bedding has been removed or when the ground is vacant. Tulips should be planted from mid-autumn onwards – too early, and any emerging new growth may be damaged by frost.

Most gardeners prefer to use a trowel, but there are special graduated bulb-planting trowels now available, which have a long narrow blade marked with measurements, which make it easier to determine the correct depth.

If you are planting bulbs in grass a hand-held bulb planter is helpful, this removes a plug of soil when pushed into the ground. The bulb is inserted and the plug replaced; it is a much quicker method when large numbers are involved.

When planting, ensure the base of the bulb is in contact with the ground, as air pockets result in the roots failing to develop.

PERENNIALS, ALPINES, FERNS AND ORNAMENTAL GRASSES

These are all plants that, although not woody, will survive and provide you with colour and interest from year to year. Familiar perennials with a preference for acid conditions include bugle (*Ajuga*), which tolerates a level of pH4.0; as well as lupins (*Lupinus*), golden rod (*Solidago*), wood lilies (*Trillium*) and forms of *Veronica*. Alpine plants such as *Androsace* and *Pulsatilla*, ferns such as the ladder fern (*Nephrolepis*) and grasses such as *Molinia*, are all acid-lovers too.

In most cases, after four or five years it is recommended that you lift the plants out of the ground, split – or divide – them, and then replant them. This not only stops the plant from getting too large and cumbersome, but also gives it a new lease of life (for you would only replant the healthiest and most vigorous portions).

ABOVE **Choose your perennial plants carefully. It is not necessarily the biggest plants that are the best as, once planted, they may take a while to start growing properly.**

ABOVE **Few sights in a garden are better than a traditional, mature herbaceous border. These days the term 'mixed' border is more appropriate as borders tend to include bedding, shrubs and bulbs as well as the usual perennial plants.**

ABOVE **Lupins are a good, old-fashioned favourite perennial, and they are perfect for an acid soil.**

Division in this way also is a form of propagation, so from one 'mother' plant you could end up with anything from two to twenty plants, depending on what it is and how big it has become.

Buying Perennials are nearly all sold in pots (the exception is when you are buying by mail order, as roots are wrapped in moist peat or other material to be sent out). When at the garden centre buy the best plants you can find. Look for vigorous, healthy and young specimens, as these will tend to establish and grow away quickly. You should not, however, buy the largest plants you see necessarily: these may be pot bound and will take time to establish. If you do end up buying a perennial plant that is pot bound, at planting time gently tease out as many of the roots from the congested 'ball' of root as possible, but try not to damage them too much.

Ideally, perennials should be planted in the spring or autumn; the spring-flowering types (such as forms of *Primula* and *Trillium*) are best planted in the autumn so that they have a chance to settle in before flowering.

Planting Water the plants, whilst they are still in their pots, an hour or two before planting them. For each plant dig a hole that is large enough to accommodate the entire root system. Depending on the size of the plant this will require using a trowel or a spade. Carefully remove the plant from its container and, if possible, spread out the roots as you place the plant in the hole. Set the crown of the plant at soil level, then back fill, firm and water in the plant.

ABOVE **When planting a perennial it is a good idea to dig the hole several times the size of the plant's root ball ...**

ABOVE **... then add a peat (or peat-alternative) planting mixture to the hole in order to help get the roots established.**

TREES, SHRUBS AND CLIMBERS

Trees and shrubs form the backbone of a garden, and without any of them a garden would appear unusual – everything would be low down, and stems and foliage would be soft and wavy; there would be no firm 'substance' to the garden. Trees favouring acid conditions include the strawberry tree (*Arbutus*), which can tolerate a level of pH4.0; the monkey puzzle (*Araucaria*), hawthorns (*Crataegus*) and spruce (*Picea*). Apart from members of the *Erica* family, other acid-loving shrubs include broom (*Cytisus*), St John's wort (*Hypericum*), holly (*Ilex*) and blue hydrangeas (the pink forms require slightly more alkaline conditions to keep the pink colour – see pages 140–41). And as far as climbers are concerned, Jasmine (*Jasminum*), *Clematis* and some forms of rambling rose can all thrive in soils with a pH of 5.5.

Buying Most trees, shrubs and climbers are already growing in pots at the garden centre, but try to make sure that they are genuine container-grown plants, not bare-root specimens that have recently been potted up. You can tell if shrubs have been in their containers for the proper length of time by moss or algae on the soil surface. Another way to identify how long a plant has been in a pot is to see if the roots are beginning to push through the holes in the base of the pot. Most importantly, however, you should ask. If you go to a reliable nursery the staff there should be able to give you accurate information.

Some woody plants are sold as 'bare-root' plants (where they have been grown in the ground at the nursery, rather than in pots).

ABOVE **Mixed Japanese acers, as seen here, can make a fabulous statement in an acid-soil garden.**

ABOVE Traditional trees, shrubs and conifers can look amazing in the right setting – helped by a natural-looking pond.

ABOVE Hybrid clematis are one of the few climbers that generally prefer an acid soil. This cultivar is 'Warszawska Nike'.

ABOVE The monkey puzzle tree (*Araucaria araucana*) usually grows very well on an acid soil.

Woody plants are usually are sold in smaller plant nurseries, through the thriving mail-order plant businesses and in stores and supermarkets. In the case of the latter two, these bare-root plants are pre-packed and sealed, usually with some moisture kept around the roots by packing in moist tissue paper, or a small amount of compost.

If you really know what you are looking for, it is possible to get excellent plants in this way, and they are usually cheaper than container-grown types because you are not buying the pot and soil. You also have the advantage of seeing if the plant has a well-developed root system. Beware, however, of those with wrinkled, dried-up stems, or premature growth caused by high temperatures in transit, or in the shop, where the transparent packaging has created a mini 'greenhouse' around the plants, causing them to grow prematurely. This can also be a very good indication of the length of time the plant has been packed, and out of the ground.

The hot atmosphere of a shop itself is rarely ideal – which is why cut-flower florists are usually very cool places – so it is sensible to buy any such bare-root shrubs within just a few days of them appearing on the shelves.

Saleable plants should have a really good, fibrous root system, and a minimum of two strong, firm shoots, no thinner than a pencil, but preferably thicker.

ABOVE **When planting acid-loving shrubs, such as an azalea, first check that the hole is big enough to accommodate the root ball.**

ABOVE **Fill the area around the roots with acid garden soil, or mix in peat or peat substitute if the soil is neutral.**

ABOVE **Make sure you firm the plant in position, and do not be afraid to use your feet for this – but don't damage the roots.**

ABOVE **Finish the planting by placing a moisture-retaining mulch, such as shredded bark, over the surface of the soil.**

Planting Late autumn is the ideal time for planting bare-root plants, and this is when many nurseries and garden centres will be stocked to capacity with them. For the vast majority the soil needs to be free-draining, but moisture-retentive. Ideally you should incorporate plenty of humus into the soil prior to planting. Mix it well into the soil around and within the planting hole; do not plant right into this material, as it is too strong for the plants' fine root hairs and will burn them. Just before you set the plants in the ground, apply a dressing of bonemeal fertilizer over the area, at the rate of 2oz per sq yd (65g per m²). Work it into the surface of the soil, using a hoe or rake, tread the area firm and then rake it level.

Setting a climbing plant against a wall usually requires you to plant it 12in (30cm) or so away from the wall, in order to avoid the footings.

ABOVE **A greenhouse can be used, during the summer months at least, as a display house for all kinds of ornamental and productive plants – and many of these can be acid-lovers.**

Container-grown trees, shrubs or climbers can be planted at any time of year, but if you are planting in summer, or during a period of hot weather in spring or autumn, you must make sure to check for watering, almost on a daily basis, until such time as the general soil is consistently moist.

Do not be fooled into thinking that, just because container-grown plants have a neat root ball when removed from the pot, you simply drop it into a dug hole. On a heavy clay soil you would be inadvertently creating a sump from which water would be slow to drain, and this could cause the roots to rot. It is a good idea, therefore, to break up the surrounding soil, and the base of the hole at planting time. Firm the plant in position and water it in.

Finally, a stake should be used to support small trees, and it should be driven into the hole before planting, so as to avoid damaging the plant's roots. To avoid unnecessary rubbing, the top of the stake should come up just to the base of the first outward branches.

HOUSE AND CONSERVATORY PLANTS

Not all of us have a garden – and many don't even have a porch or balcony. But all of us, without exception, can keep houseplants. They are included here as it is not just outdoor plants that have preferences for acid or alkaline soils. Indoor and greenhouse plants are just as demanding, but because we nearly always grow them in containers, either keep them in the pots that they arrived in, or we re-pot them using multi-purpose bagged compost, we don't tend to think so much about their soil requirements.

A conservatory gives us the best opportunity for growing indoor plants, as it provides copious amounts of daylight, the lack of which can often be the death knell of some indoor plants, especially cacti and succulents.

But which plants are acid-lovers? The cast iron plant (*Aspidistra*), Venus fly trap (*Dionaea*), mother-in-law's tongue (*Sansevieria*) and most cacti and succulents require acidic conditions if they are to do well. See the A–Z Directory (pages 152–55) for more details and descriptions.

VEGETABLES AND FRUITS

Those of us with an acid soil, and who want to grow their own food, should not worry. Fortunately there is a good number of types that tolerate and even prefer acid conditions. And if your soil is alkaline, then most food crops can also be grown in large tubs and containers with imported acid topsoil.

Vegetable crops most desiring of acid soil include potatoes, carrots, chicory, fennel peppers, shallots, swedes and turnips. Acid loving fruits include apples, blackberries, figs, gooseberries, raspberries, melons and citrus. And a number of herbs like an acid soil too; these include parsley, rosemary, basil, chives, sage and thyme. (See also A–Z Directory, pages 140–51.)

ABOVE **Indoor plants do, of course, grow outdoors in their usually warmer native countries, and most of them also have natural preferences for acidic or alkaline soils.**

ABOVE **The fruit and vegetable, or 'kitchen' garden will be home to many acid- or alkaline-loving plants, and it pays to know what soil you have so that you do not waste your time and effort growing the types of plant that will never reap good harvests.**

CHAPTER 5

Maintenance of plants

Garden plants need a certain amount of care and attention if they are to give the best displays for our pleasure, and acid-loving plants are no exception. Watering, feeding, weeding and pruning are by far the most important considerations, but pest and disease control is also vital to get right.

ABOVE **Looking after your acid-loving plants involves watering them in times of drought, as well as feeding them, weeding them, pruning them, staking them and controlling any pests and diseases that infect them.**

WATERING

All plants need water to survive – and grow – and it is important never to allow them to dry out completely. Even the cacti found in deserts across the world need water to survive; they take in what little moisture is available and they store it within the flesh of the plant, to use when times get hard.

After you have planted up your acid-soil garden, watering is essential until the new plants have become established, and this could take two, or even three, years. Even then you should always water your plants during hot and dry spells.

Watering is best carried out either early in the day or in the evening – both times when evaporation will be at its slowest, avoiding the heat of the day. Remember also, a good soaking of the soil every few days is better for plants – and less wasteful of water – than a mere splash around the leaves and stems twice a day.

FEEDING

Plants growing in an acid soil, which very often is sandy and free-draining, are likely to need more feeding than those growing in heavier clay, or chalk soils. And plants grown directly in the ground will require less feeding than those growing in pots or containers.

The best course of action is to provide annual mulches of manure in early spring. As well as helping to retain soil moisture, this will feed the plants. Between mulches it is a good idea to supplement the feeding by applying liquid, granular or pelleted fertilizer. If you want to buy some plant fertilizer, and you don't know exactly what you want – prepare to be baffled!

Yes, there are foods for indoor plants, container plants, trees, shrubs and lawns; there are foods to promote flowering, fruiting, leaf production and root formation. There are granules, powders and liquids, some ready-to-use, and others that need mixing. There are tablets for aquatic plants, and granule clusters for container plants.

ABOVE **Watering plants when they are dry is the most importing job of all. A plant can generally be revived if it gets hungry, but there is a much greater chance that it will die if it dries out.**

ABOVE **The watering can take the form of sophisticated hose-end sprays and nozzles, or you can simply use a finger over the end to create a spray.**

ABOVE **Feeding – here with a granular fertilizer – should only take place when the plants are in active growth.**

There are ericaceous fertilizers (for lime-hating plants), and others formulated for roses, tomatoes, African violets, bonsai, citrus plants and cacti. There are quick-fix feeds and slow-release feeds, and there are 'organic' feeds and 'inorganic' feeds.

After half an hour of this you are probably ready to run screaming from the shop, but really it's not that difficult to understand. Happy plants are healthy plants – like animals, plants must have food to provide energy for making growth.

Plants need certain nutrients, and we have met all of them so far in this book. Starting with the most important, they are carbon, oxygen, hydrogen (all three of which are obtained from the air and water in the soil), and then there is nitrogen, potassium and phosphorous (obtained from fertilizers).

Then there are the 'trace elements', which may actually be lacking in some gardens, causing plants to go yellow, become stunted, or be flowerless. These are (again in order of importance) calcium, magnesium, sulphur, sodium, iron, manganese, zinc, copper and finally, molybdenum. Without any of these 15 elements, plants will perform poorly, become susceptible to all kinds of pests and diseases or, in extreme cases, cease to live completely.

'Balanced' or 'general' fertilizers contain roughly equal proportions of nitrogen, phosphates and potash, and are of use to all plants. The high-potash types (including most rose and tomato fertilizers) boost flower and fruit growth, and high-nitrogen types assist the growth of foliage – important in the case of variegated plants and leaf vegetables.

It is strongly advisable to follow a programme of applying these general fertilizers during the year. The good news is that you need only apply the trace element fertilizers if you have identified that your soil is lacking one or more of those lesser nutrients. The only really hard-and-fast rule is to feed plants when they are in active growth. Essentially, this means that if you feed

outdoor plants between, say, mid-autumn and mid-winter, the rains will wash most of the fertilizer away. The plants are either dormant during these months, or their growth rates are so slow that they are unable to take up goodness from the soil.

Generally, the most beneficial time to feed plants is just at the beginning of their annual growing cycle, using a good growth-boosting feed, and then one or more times during the season with flower- or fruit-producing feeds. Anything in addition to this is a bonus.

As far as liquid feeds are concerned, unless it states 'ready-to-use' on the side of the packet or container, they are usually going to be in concentrated form, and they will need diluting in a watering can or sprayer. The important thing is always to read the instructions, not only about how to apply the fertilizer, but also as regards the dosage. You can more quickly kill a plant by overfeeding it than by neglecting it.

DISORDERS CAUSED BY CULTURAL CONDITIONS

Acid-lovers – such as rhododendrons, azaleas, camellias and heathers – are specific in their requirements. Feed the plants with fertilizers that are specially formulated for ericaceous plants, and there are several on the market.

Sometimes plants can appear very sickly, yet they are not infected by any pest or disease at all. Such plants are likely to be suffering from a lack of specific foods (minerals, nutrients and elements). They could also be growing in the wrong kind of soil (an acid-loving plant in an alkaline soil is, of course, the most relevant example).

A deficiency of a mineral can vary, depending on the plant and the mineral in question. The *Camellia* seen in the picture opposite has been growing on an alkaline soil. This has generally caused the plant to be tardy in growth, with an overall dull yellowish colour rather than a rich green.

ABOVE This *Camellia* has been weakened by being grown on an alkaline soil, and this has made it susceptible to other disorders.

ABOVE It is particularly important to keep a vegetable garden weed-free, as the crops will not need to compete for nutrients, moisture and light with the weeds.

More importantly the plant is weak, which has meant that it has become susceptible to wind and frost damage, and this in time manifests as scorching and spotting.

In most cases the cure is to make sure the plants are well fed but, fundamentally, you should also make sure that the plant is suitable to the soil.

WEEDING

Keep your garden as free from weeds as possible. Unfortunately there is no simple, magical cure for the problem of weeds, just remember that by allowing them to grow, you will be causing your treasured plants to compete for moisture, food, light and space. Many weeds also become host plants for the breeding of aphids, and others make the ideal homes for diseases like mildew and rust. There are many reasons, therefore, to control weeds.

The easiest weeds to control are annuals, which are best kept in check by hoeing, mulching and spraying. The more troublesome weeds, however, are the perennial weeds, such as ground elder, couch grass (or twitch), bindweed, docks, thistles and perennial nettles. These will all come up year after year if left to their own devices.

ABOVE Perennial weeds, such as thistles, can be difficult to control and often the most effective method is to remove them by hand.

ABOVE Removing perennial weeds should be carried out on a regular basis, otherwise they will flower, set seed and spread, or spread via their networks of roots.

59

Initial clearing When you are first setting out plants in your acid soil, you should make sure that the ground is completely weed-free. This is particularly important if there are present perennial weeds, such as those mentioned on the previous page. If you have an area covered with, for example, couch grass, the best course of action is to spray the area with a herbicide based on glyphosate, which will kill all parts of the plant it is sprayed on to. It becomes inactive on contact with the soil, and it is not taken up by the roots of any plant, no matter how close to the area of spray.

Controlling weed germination To control new weed seedlings from appearing amongst the plants in your garden, use only those products, probably based on simazine, that carry the manufacturer's recommendations for use with ornamental or edible plants. Apply in spring, when the soil is firm and moist. The chemical acts as a sort of sealant over the soil, preventing weed seeds from germinating. It should remain active for the whole growing season.

Before applying, remove any weeds by hand. Or, if they are very small, hoe lightly or apply a contact weedkiller such as paraquat – but be careful to avoid letting this chemical come into contact with the plants you are growing. Prune and feed the plants as required and only then should you apply the simazine-based control. Finish off by applying a mulch.

Perennial weed control Any weed can be removed by hand, but it is the perennial kinds that really should be controlled in this way. Dig out as much of the root as possible. However, if there are large areas covered with them, or they are growing in between dangerously spiked plants (hollies, roses, pyracanthas, and so on), you could spray with a weedkiller based on dichlobenil. Apply it when the soil is moist, and in early spring before growth gets under way.

Some perennial weeds (such as couch grass and ground elder) will be checked or controlled but other, deeper-rooting weeds, may not be checked sufficiently to kill them off, so hand-weeding is best for these.

Dichlobenil will also control germinating weed seedlings and established annual weeds for up to six months after application.

If grass weeds are your main problem, apply a weedkiller based on alloxydim-sodium. It is foliage-acting, non-residual and harmless to non-grassy plants, so it will not matter if you inadvertently get some on your woody plants.

ABOVE **Chickweed is a common annual weed. It is frustrating to pull by hand, however, as it usually breaks off above soil level.**

ABOVE **Dandelions are perennial weeds. If you pull them or hoe them off, the roots remaining in the ground will grow again.**

ABOVE **Fabric mulches are available, and these are used most effectively in kitchen gardens, where the view of the fabric will be less important.**

ABOVE **Pruning some vigorous plants (such as *Wisteria*, seen here), means that they remain manageable, and within bounds.**

Fabric mulches These are widely available these days. They are generally black, brown or white and they are purely functional in that they are designed to suppress weeds and keep moisture in the soil; they are not supposed to look attractive. Therefore they are almost always used in a kitchen garden where the aesthetics are not so important as the keeping down of weeds. These fabric mulches may, of course, be used in an ornamental setting, but in such situations they are generally used as a weed-preventer on the soil and under a more attractive layer of gravel or shredded bark.

PRUNING

There are several reasons why we prune plants:

Keeping to size Most of us have smaller gardens than our ancestors enjoyed, so it has become essential either to select and grow plants that will achieve a modest size when fully grown, or to limit the size of larger subjects by keeping them under control. In other words, pruning them carefully so that they do not grow too big.

Maintaining shape Most trees and shrubs look at their best when they are allowed to grow naturally; trained plants, or those trimmed to a

ABOVE **One of the reasons we prune plants is to keep them in shape – or to create an artificial yet interesting shape, such as the rounded pyramid of this yew tree (*Taxus baccata*).**

formal shape, are exceptions to this. But awkwardly placed shoots will upset the balance occasionally and, in such circumstances, these growths should be cut out.

First, remove straggling branches to a shoot or bud within the main bulk of the plant; second, carefully but systematically reduce the number of growths on the 'good' side of the plant; third, cut back weak shoots hard, and strong shoots lightly on the 'bad' side of the plant. Follow by feeding, mulching and watering, and your plants will repay you manifold.

ABOVE Most ornamental flowering shrubs, including *Fuchsia*, produce more and better flowers if the plants undergo an annual pruning regime.

ABOVE If pruning is carried out to improve flowering, in the case of fruiting trees and shrubs this will also mean that they produce heavier and better crops.

Improve flowering Pruning at the right time of year, and to a bud, can increase the quantity and quality of flowering, particularly if the pruning regime is accompanied by feeding and watering when required. As we have seen, some acid soils can lack plant nutrients, so anything to help plants on such impoverished soils becomes of greater importance.

Usually, the more flowers a plant produces, the smaller they become. Pruning therefore reduces the amount of wood, and so diverts energy into the production of appreciably larger, though fewer, flowers. Decoration is what gardening is all about!

Improve fruiting Flowers usually lead to fruit, so if you are wanting to maximize a plant's potential for fruiting, more or less the same pruning guidelines as for flowering plants apply: to continually aim to encourage productive growth. With our fruiting plants we generally want the largest possible crops, but there can come a time when the plant bears too many fruits, all of which are small. Larger fruits can be achieved if the crop is thinned out well before ripening – another form of pruning.

Improve foliage and stems Certainly, where deciduous plants are concerned, leaves are produced only on the current season's growth, so the more vigorous this is, the larger and more profuse will be the foliage. Also, in plants with coloured leaves, the hues will be more intense. For this reason, many vigorous shrubs grown for their foliage are pruned hard annually.

Green shoots on plants that are variegated should be cut out, right to their bases. These reverted growths tend to be more vigorous than the rest of the plant, and if left to their own devices will take over, spoiling the overall appearance of the plant.

Some deciduous shrubs, such as *Cornus alba* (dogwood), *Salix alba vitellina* (willow) and *Rubus cockburnianus* (white-stemmed bramble), have coloured stems, and are grown purposely to enhance the winter garden. The most effective colour is produced on young stems, so these shrubs should be cut as close to the ground as possible in early spring.

Remove unwanted growth Plants that are not looked after can become a dense mass of tangled branches. This means that the shoots in

ABOVE There are a number of plants that are grown for their decorative or productive stems – *Rubus thibetanus*, seen here, has attractive white stems in winter, whilst another example would be the raspberry. Both types of plant need to be pruned annually so that there is an annual batch of fresh stems.

DEADHEADING

All cultivated flowering plants should be dead-headed – the removal of faded flowers before the plant has created the seed which follows. By doing this you are saving the plant a huge amount of wasted energy. Deadheading can either encourage more flowers in the same year, or help to build up the plant for better flowering the following year.

Generally, the recommendation for woody plants is to use a pair of secateurs, and to cut off the faded flowers, cutting the stalks down as far as the first set of leaves. As always there are exceptions. Rhododendrons, for example, should have their old flowerheads snapped off – and for this it is far better to use your fingers. Bedding plants and some soft perennials can be deadheaded and this may be best done with fingers, or a pair of shears (as you would with, say, lavender).

ABOVE Sometimes we need to prune plants just to get rid of unwanted growth. Perhaps odd shoots grow at awkward angles, whilst others may be just too long.

the middle are deprived of light and air, and are prone to dying back. During windy weather the stems can rub together, causing injury to themselves and the branches they are rubbing against. To avoid a greatly increased risk of disease, prune these branches out annually.

ABOVE Deadheading plants is important if you want good flowering the following year. Rhododendrons, particularly, benefit from thorough deadheading.

ABOVE Staking and supporting some perennials is important if you want them to keep their shape and prolong their season of interest. Here, twigs are used to support soft stems.

ABOVE Plant diseases – such as the fungal grey-mould disease (*Botrytis*) – can spoil a whole garden, or a whole season, but many can be prevented, and some can be cured.

STAKING AND SUPPORTING

Many herbaceous plants that grow away again each spring will require some form of support to prevent them flopping over other plants, or in on themselves. Tie them to bamboo canes, or buy purpose-made wire hoop supports that are pushed in the ground for the plant to grow up and through. These should be put in position in the early to mid-spring period, before the plants start growing apace.

As new stems on climbing plants develop, they should be tied in to wires or trelliswork, to avoid wind damage. If this is done regularly, they should be in position to replace any older wood that needs to be pruned out at the appropriate pruning time. Left untied they may break, or get in the way and they will certainly look untidy.

PESTS AND DISEASES

Acid-loving plants are prone to just the same sorts of problems as plants growing in any other kind of soil. And, although they need an acidic soil in order to perform in the optimum way, just like any other plant, they are vulnerable occasionally to pest and disease attack.

Fortunately plant breeders have worked hard over the years to bring us plants resistant to certain diseases. Also, these days there are some very effective controls available.

INSECT PESTS

Amongst a plethora of insect pests that attack our garden plants, these are the most common:

Aphids These are the familiar greenfly and blackfly, and are found worldwide, infesting a wide range of plants. They feed by sucking the sap of young, tender shoots, and they are often seen clustering on young, unopened buds, and on the undersides of young leaves. Their feeding will not kill an established plant, unless it is very small, but it will distort the buds and leaves, and reduce flowering and fruiting potential. They can also spread diseases and viruses.

Small infestations should be cut off the plants and discarded. For larger infestations there are many suitable insecticides available (some of them organic in nature, which means that organic gardeners who do not wish to spray with man-made pesticides, can have a form of mass control).

ABOVE **Blackfly can be a real problem on certain ornamental and edible plants. Fortunately they are relatively easily controlled with organic and chemical sprays.**

ABOVE **There are dozens of different types of caterpillar – the larval stages of certain moths and butterflies – that are harmful to plants. There are sprays available to control most of them.**

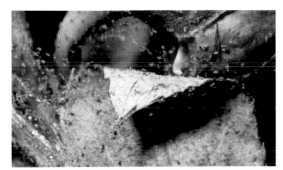

ABOVE **Red spider mites – little spiders that are actually rather more yellow than red – produce very fine webbing in plant crevices; the pest is more troublesome in hot, dry weather.**

ABOVE **The adult vine weevil will munch its way through the leaves of many plants, whilst its grub or larval stage will also attack roots underground, out of sight of the gardener.**

Red spider mites Attacks from this pest are worst in hot, dry weather. They attack the leaves and stems of a wide range of plants, and not always the soft, sappy growths that are generally favoured by aphids. Bronze patches on the upper surfaces of leaves are typical symptoms of red spider mite presence. You will probably see very fine, silky webbing between the leaves and stems. The spiders are tiny and yellowish rather than red. Chemical control is possible and there is a good range of pesticides available.

Caterpillars A number of different caterpillar species will readily devour foliage. One of the worst is the caterpillar of the winter moth, which is bright green and some ½in (1cm) long. If they are not too numerous, pick them off by hand. Otherwise, spray with a suitable insecticide.

Vine weevils This pest is marginally less troublesome on an acid soil, and it is mainly a pest of plants growing in large tubs and containers (although it is known to affect garden plants as well).

The grubs of the vine weevil eat into the roots and plants wilt and die in the period between autumn and spring. During summer the adult weevils eat irregular-shaped holes in leaf margins, and they'll be laying their eggs.

The main control available to gardeners is a chemical called imidacloprid, which is available in various formulations for spraying on to plants, or impregnated in potting compost as a preventative.

Earwigs These are an important pest of dahlias and chrysanthemums. At night the petals are eaten, making them ragged and unsightly by morning. During the day the earwigs hide in the heart of the blooms or beneath leaves and other debris on the ground. Clearing away garden rubbish can have a surprisingly beneficial effect; but there are also sprays available.

Capsid bugs Similar plants are affected, but these insects are sapsuckers. They may kill flower buds or, if they do open, the blooms develop lop-sided. Sprays are available.

NON-INSECT PESTS

Sadly it seems there are as many different types of non-insect pests.

Slugs and snails The slug frequently ranks as the number one offender for gardeners. The snail has a hard shell, but otherwise is as troublesome. Both molluscs inhabit dark, cool, moist places such as under pots or stones.

They will readily munch their way through the soft, fleshy leaves and stems of seedlings, as well as many types of bedding plants and soft perennials – marigolds and hostas are arguably the best-known delicacies for these pests.

Granular baits based on metaldehyde or methiocarb can be applied in small quantities to the ground near to susceptible plants, but I prefer to use less toxic remedies. I have tried the old wives' tales of putting down orange peel (which attracts them in numbers where they can be collected and disposed of in a manner of your choosing) and also beer traps, where they are lured into a slop-trough of beer, get drunk and drown. I have also tried the biological controls –

ABOVE **Snails like to hide in cool, damp, shady places, such as behind containers. This colony of snails was discovered when a trough was moved. When so many are gathered in one place, hand picking is the only way to control them.**

ABOVE **Slugs – and snails – can be controlled with one of the baits commonly available. There are also a number of organic options, the latest being nematodes which you apply to the soil; they enter the slugs and kill them from within.**

nematodes that you water onto the soil. All can work, and sometimes well, but there are never any guarantees.

Birds These will eat fruits and berries; blackbirds can strip a holly tree of berries in a matter of a few hours. Other birds break in to ripening apples and pears hanging on the trees, and others eat flower buds just before they burst open.

Netting, either draped over vulnerable plants, or in the form of a structured 'fruit cage', are the only guaranteed ways to control them. Bird scarers work with mixed success.

I believe, however, that we should encourage birds into our gardens as some (most notably thrushes) will eat slugs and snails. Others (including many of the sparrows and tit families) consume aphids and other small crawlers.

Mammals Rabbits, deer and voles are regular garden pests, especially in a rural setting. During spring, rabbits will frequently devour young and emerging perennial plants. Deer will eat stems, buds, leaves and bark of young trees.

ABOVE **Birds can cause immense damage to a crop of apples, and they can strip raspberry and blackberry canes of fruit in a very short period of time.**

Voles cause damage similar to that caused by deer, but much lower down, nearer to the ground. Tree guards, made from plastic and usually in green, brown or white, and metal tree protectors are useful for keeping the larger animals away. Special low vole guards are also available to stop these rodents.

ABOVE **Rabbits will eat a wide range of soft plants, and they can strip young trees of their bark; damage is usually worst in the spring.**

ABOVE Rhododendron 'bud blast' is a disease that straddles the pest-and-disease spectrum. Although a fungal disease it is, in the main, spread by the leafhopper insect.

ABOVE Mildew, seen here on a rose, is probably the worst and most widespread fungal disease of garden plants. Plants that are stressed (hungry or dry) are more susceptible to it.

Rhododendron 'bud blast' This is a disease that straddles the pest-and-disease spectrum. Although a fungal disease it is, in the main, spread by the leafhopper insect. Apply a special spray to control the insect in late summer; this will reduce the likelihood of the leafhopper puncturing holes in the developing *Rhododendron* buds. The disease spores enter through these holes.

If your rhododendrons develop buds with a dry, brown appearance, and they fail to grow but stay in place without dropping, then the disease has taken hold and all you can do is to remove and destroy the affected buds. Some varieties of *Rhododendron* are claimed to be more resistant to 'bud blast' than others, but in my experience this hasn't been the case.

PLANT DISEASES

There are a number of ailments that befall our plants and they cannot always be blamed on insects, mammals or birds. As with human biology, plant diseases fall into three different categories: fungal, viral and bacterial. It is the first, by far, that causes most problems.

Fungal Spores of a fungus can travel across the garden carried on the wind, through the soil or via water flow. The biological aim for these spores is to settle and infect new areas. Honey fungus, for example, is a disease that can kill even mature trees and shrubs; it shows a white 'mycelium', a thread-like mass of filaments or strands forming the vegetative part of the fungus. Coral spot is a disease affecting dead wood, and spreads to living wood; it is seen as, actually, quite decorative coral pink round pustules growing on the surface of the bark.

The following are probably the most widespread fungal diseases of garden plants: mildew, recognized by a white, powder-like coating on leaves. There are two different types of mildew. The most important form is 'powdery mildew', which attacks mainly the tender, younger shoots. Without treatment, the disease will cause the affected parts to become stunted and distorted. Spores are carried on the wind, and they will most readily infect plants that are slightly dehydrated, or if there is poor air circulation around the plant, such as with climbers growing against walls. The spores germinate most readily in cool, wet weather.

The second type of mildew is of lesser importance, and is known as 'downy mildew'. This is characterized by greyish-brown pustules on the undersides of the leaves.

Both can be controlled by using a suitable fungicide – control comes in the form of preventative spraying, so do not wait until you see the presence of the disease. By then it is too late.

Rust disease produces irregular discolouration that appears on leaves, and on closer inspection these are vaguely circular and correspond to dark orange, brown, yellow or red spots or pustules on the undersides of the leaves. Stems are also affected. Rust affects a wide variety of plants and some of the most severely affected are roses, chrysanthemums, pelargoniums, antirrhinums and hollyhocks, and even vegetables such as broad beans. Chemical sprays are available, but severely infected plants should be lifted and burnt.

Viral You can't cure plant viruses. Pests – particularly greenfly and eelworms – frequently spread viruses between plants, which is why it is so important to control these insects. Once infection occurs nearly every cell of a diseased plant becomes infected, and there is no method by which a gardener can cure it. The plant should destroyed, preferably by burning as this gets rid of the virus; simply putting it on the compost heap is likely spread the virus.

Bacterial A number of different strains of bacteria cause problems for plants. Infection invariably enters a plant through a wound or opening. 'Bacterial canker' is a serious disease of many forms of tree and shrub, as well as fruiting plants and even vegetables such as tomatoes and cucumbers. In woody plants symptoms include oozing gum from the bark.

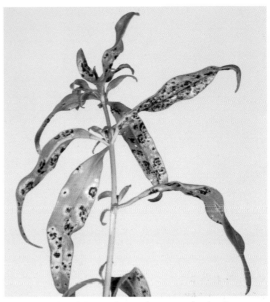

ABOVE **Rust, a fungal disease that produces irregular discolouration on leaves and often stems (here an *Antirrhimum*), can sometimes be controlled with sprays, but you will need to act quickly.**

ABOVE **This is a pear fruit – hardly recognizable as it is rotting due to a bacterial infection. As with viruses, there is no control, so you will need to destroy the whole of the infected crops.**

There are several bacterial 'spots' and 'rots' that affect a range of plants. As with the virally affected plants, there is no cure, and the individual plants may need to be destroyed. In the case of trees and shrubs, it may be possible to cut out the affected parts and to seal over the wounds with protective sealants, but success is not guaranteed.

CHAPTER 6

Year-round care

ABOVE **In early winter dig over the soil in vegetable gardens, or new beds; incorporate plenty of organic matter as you go.**

ABOVE **Remove dead, diseased, damaged or crossing wood from bush roses; make the cut just above a bud, facing outwards from the plant.**

EARLY WINTER

Soil preparation: If the weather is mild, start planning any changes to beds and borders. Areas to be planted with long-term shrubs and perennials should be dug over and plenty of organic matter incorporated into the top 18in (45cm) of soil. The soil needs time to settle, so do not do any planting yet. When the ground is not frozen, mulch shrubs and border plants with well-rotted bulky manure or garden compost.

Planting: However, new hardy shrubs may be planted, on a day when the soil is not frozen or waterlogged, on ground prepared a month or two previously. But before you dig the holes and plant them, give the area a final application of bonemeal fertilizer at 2oz per sq yd (65g per m²), working this into the surface, treading the ground firm and then raking it level.

Heathers: Plant winter-flowering heathers in gaps in borders where colour is lacking. If your soil is alkaline, plunge the pots, and lift them when flowering is over.

MID-WINTER

Shrubs in pots: Bring potted camellias, azaleas and rhododendrons into a conservatory or cool, well-lit room, to force early flowers.

Prick over bulb beds: Spring bulbs will be appearing through the soil now. Go over the beds carefully with a small border fork, pricking the soil between the bulbs, but only to the depth of about 1in (2.5cm). This improves aeration, kills moss and loosens weeds for removal.

Pruning roses: Climbing roses, hybrid tea and floribunda bush roses may be pruned, but leave ramblers until late summer. The aim should be to keep five to seven strong shoots, spaced well apart, and to tie them in well. Remove as many as possible of the older stems that have flowered.

Indoor potted azaleas: By now these plants will have gone past their best, so it is time to nip off the spent blooms; this will prevent the plant from wasting its energy in the production of seedpods.

ABOVE **Prune mophead hydrangeas in late winter, as the faded brown flowers are still quite attractive and help protect the plant.**

ABOVE **If perennial plants become congested after a few years, and flowering starts to decline, divide them in early spring.**

LATE WINTER

Plant heathers: Forms of *Erica, Calluna* and *Daboecia* should be planted now.

Prune flowering shrubs: Acid-loving flowering shrubs which should be pruned now include climbing hydrangea (*Hydrangea petiolaris*), the Rose of Sharon (*Hypericum calycinum*) and colour-stemmed dogwood (*Cornus alba*). Stems made the previous year should be cut hard back to within one or two joints of the older wood.

Prune hydrangeas: When mophead hydrangeas finish flowering at the end of summer do not cut off the faded flowerheads. These brown heads provide a degree of winter protection to the growth and flower buds. Instead, they can be removed now, just before the new buds swell. The rest of the hydrangea can be pruned as well, but not a severe cut.

Control rabbits: Damage to your trees and shrubs by rabbits can be very significant, particularly if you live in a rural area. The main damage is caused to the fresh growths that emerge after pruning. You may wish to erect a barrier of wire netting, some 3ft (90cm) high, around your plants and/or rose bed at this time. Turn the bottom 6in (15cm) of the wire mesh outwards, and bury it under the soil or turf. This will help to safeguard your plants. It is advisable to leave the barrier in place until the worst of the rabbit activity is past (after about two months).

EARLY SPRING

Apply fertilizer: Plants set out in well-manured soil do not require a dressing of fertilizer in spring. Established plants, however, should be given a feed, using a balanced fertilizer. Always check the application rates on the side of the packet. Rake or hoe the feed into the top inch or two of the soil.

Dividing plants: This is the best time to transplant the majority of herbaceous plants. When transplanting old clumps always break them up into smaller pieces, and if you have plenty of stock throw away the hard central portions, keeping only the outside pieces. This is particularly important for plants that get less attractive as they age, such as golden rod (*Solidago*), wake robin (*Trillium grandiflorum*) and forms of *Campanula*. Chives, growing in the vegetable or herb garden, can also be split at this time.

Get your compost straight: This is a good time to get the compost heap in order. A compost heap should be positioned directly on to the ground. A heap (or an enclosure) about 3ft (1m) square at the base and around 4ft (1.2m) high, should be suitable for most gardens.

Pests and diseases: Look for early aphids and control them. These insects breed at an alarming rate unless they are spotted at an early stage and action taken immediately.

ABOVE Tackle weeds as soon as possible once the weather starts to warm up – here weedkiller is being applied to a gravel area.

ABOVE Removing the faded flowers from daffodils and other spring bulbs and shrubs will encourage more blooms the following year.

MID-SPRING

Weeding: By starting a regime of control now, much can be done to minimize the time spent on weeding later in the year: i) do not let weeds get to the seeding stage. Groundsel, chickweed and bittercress flower and seed very quickly, so pull them out as soon as you see them; ii) hoe soil even if there are no weeds present. It will kill any weed seeds in the process of germinating; iii) a 4in (10cm) thick mulch of compost or shredded bark will go a long way to smothering weed growth; iv) when tackling deep-rooted perennial weeds, like dandelions, docks and thistles, make sure you get every piece of root out, otherwise they'll continue growing; v) attack weeds in paving and gravel paths as well.

Feed lawns: Grass on an acid soil is under stress, so it is important also to aerate the soil – spiking the area with a garden fork to a depth of about 6in (15cm). This is particularly important under large trees. Feed the grass twice a year: now, using a proprietary lawn fertilizer formulated for spring/summer use, and again in the autumn.

Pot-grown shrubs: Acid-loving plants, such as camellias and azaleas, can be moved on to larger pots, in ericaceous compost, once their flowering has finished. Otherwise, just top dress them with fresh compost or fine bark chippings.

LATE SPRING

Deadhead camellias and spring bulbs: Snap off dead daffodil blooms, and pick off faded camellias. Most other spring flowers can be similarly treated.

Propagate by layering: This is a simple method of propagating quite a lot of acid-loving plants, including rhododendrons and magnolias. Choose a good, supple branch or stem, preferably one formed the previous year; make an upward incision through one of its joints, not too near the tip but at a point that can easily be bent down to soil level, press the cut portion of the stem into the soil (or a pot filled with cuttings compost), and hold it in position with a wire peg or heavy stone. After six to eight months roots should have formed and this section can then be severed from the main plant.

Tie-in climbers: As new stems develop, tie in to their supports, to avoid wind damage. If this is done regularly, they should be in position to replace the older wood, which can be pruned out during the following mid-winter. Left untied they may well break, or at least be inflexible enough to make tying in later on more difficult.

Plant up containers: Plant up summer-flowering annuals in hanging baskets and patio planters.

Pests and diseases: Continue to look out for signs of infestation or infection: never let them gain a firm hold. Spray as necessary.

AROVE **The regal lily (*Lilium regale*) makes a stunning display in pots and has a heavenly fragrance.**

AROVF Mid-summer is a good time to cut back shrubs such as rosemary (*Rosmarinus officinalis*) before it grows too large for its space.

EARLY SUMMER

Pests and diseases: Aphids will be troublesome around now. The larvae of various caterpillars eat leaf, stem and flower tissue, reducing them to skeletons. Red spider mite can infect fruit trees as this time. For all these pests you should spray now. Also, spray the top and undersides of leaves with a fungicide as a precaution against mildew. Once the white mildew appears, spraying is ineffective.

Feeding: Unless your soil is particularly fertile, established plants will benefit from another application of fertilizer. A balanced, general feed at the rate of 2 oz per sq yd (65g per m²) will encourage blooms. Do not apply this feed beyond early summer, as it will promote growth of young stems that will not ripen before the onset of colder weather.

Hedges: Evergreen hedges can be trimmed now that nesting birds have moved on.

Lilies in pots: Plant some *Lilium regale* – to my mind the most majestic of all lilies. It is a highly perfumed lily and one of the easiest to grow, and I think it is far better suited to container-growing than out in the border. Good drainage is essential. The container must be at least 12in (30cm) deep to accommodate the roots. You can grow three bulbs in a pot this deep and the same across.

MID-SUMMER

Prune flowering shrubs: Any shrubs that flowered during mid- to late spring can be pruned now, but this is not to say that pruning is always necessary. Much depends upon the purpose for which the shrub is being grown and the amount of space that you can spare it. Lilacs, rhododendrons, azaleas, pieris and camellias do not particularly need regular pruning.

Trimming perennials and shrubs: *Aubrieta*, *Arabis* and *Iberis* (perennial candytuft) may be cut back quite considerably as soon as they have finished flowering if you wish to prevent the plants from spreading very far. Similarly rosemary (*Rosmarinus*) and early-flowering lavender can be given a light trim to keep them both from producing unnecessarily long shoots.

Pests and diseases: Continue to control them. Aphids may be marginally less of a problem from now, but rose rust may be becoming evident. If you have a rhododendron, watch out for leafhopper insects which puncture the buds and set off bud blast disease. At the first sign of attack, spray with a suitable insecticide available from the garden centre.

Watering: Water plants as necessary, especially perennials and woody plants that were planted this spring. The first year of any new plant's life is the most vulnerable to 'drying out'.

ABOVE **Saving and sowing your own seed from flowering plants is fun. However, the progeny do not always look like their parents!**

ABOVE **If you want to propagate your favourite shrubs, cuttings of semi-ripe wood may be taken now.**

LATE SUMMER

Prune rambler roses: Late summer and into early autumn is the best time for pruning ramblers growing on sunless walls and fences.

Ordering new bulbs: Around now specialist bulb nurseries are bringing out their mail-order catalogues. Choose your plants and place your orders early, particularly if you are wanting newly launched varieties, as stocks may run out.

Trim hedges: Continue to trim evergreen hedges and topiary specimens as necessary to keep them neat and tidy.

Containers: Replenish containers, replacing any summer-flowering plants that may have finished, filling in gaps as you go. Make sure the containers are always well watered, and if there is a large number of flowering plants, a foliar feed with a high potash fertilizer, such as tomato feed, will help to encourage more flowers.

Saving seed: Select a few perennials or annuals and save the seed from them. Cut the seedheads off, while they are still green, and while the seedpods are swollen but before they are split. Place them in a container in a warm, dry place until the seedpods have ripened and spilled the contents. Remove any loose material from around the seeds, and store them until spring.

EARLY AUTUMN

Feed lawns: Grass that is predominately in the shade should be given its second feed of the year, using a proprietary lawn fertilizer formulated for autumn use. Before you do this, however, it makes sense to put down a mosskiller to eradicate this problem if present.

Pests and diseases: If necessary, keep spraying against pests and diseases until the mid-autumn, after which chemical controls become ineffective – both the insect pests and the fungal problems will have gone past their active life cycles.

Perennial borders: Tidy these by removing any supporting canes and storing them under cover. Cut back dead stems close to the crown. Weed the soil, and fork in natural fish, blood and bonemeal to boost growth next spring.

Propagation: Take semi-ripe cuttings of hardy garden shrubs, and root them in pots of gritty soil in a propagating frame or cold frame.

Mulching: Mulch rhododendrons and azaleas with well-rotted compost or manure.

Bulbs: Plant spring-flowering narcissi, tulips, hyacinths and others. Plant summer-flowering lily bulbs in well-worked humus-rich soil. Lift gladioli corms and dry them off in the protection of a frost-free shed.

ABOVE **Plant spring-flowering bulbs in mid-autumn. Daffodils can be planted in late summer, and tulips (shown here) up until late autumn.**

ABOVE **To make your own leafmould, gather fallen leaves and stack or bag them. A lawnmower with a grass-collecting bag is useful for this.**

MID-AUTUMN

Sow lawns: Grass seed will germinate well enough at this time, but you could also wait until spring if this is more convenient. Choose a grass seed mixture that is recommended for shade, which will probably contain wood meadow grass (*Poa nemoralis*) and fine-leaved fescue (*Festuca tenuifolia*).

Containers: Seasonal flowers in windowboxes, hanging baskets and tubs are, arguably, more important in winter than they are in summer when there is so much other colour and I always make up a few containers for winter colour around now. A small golden conifer (any kind will do, as long as it is small), white heather, a miniature rose, pink hybrid cyclamen, a trailing ivy and some silver foliage (*Senecio maritima*) can look great all winter. The bonus is that all of these can be planted out in the garden when spring arrives.

Bulbs: Continue to plant spring bulbs. Tulips and hyacinths can be planted up to late autumn.

Autumn leaves: Remove dead leaves from flowerbeds, rockeries, lawns and footpaths. If left to rot in place they will harm, or even kill, the plants or grass beneath them. On paths they can become slippery and dangerous. Burn leaves if mildew or rust was present during the previous growing season.

LATE AUTUMN

Make leafmould: Broad-leaved (as opposed to coniferous) deciduous trees are shedding their leaves now. To make your own leafmould make a 'leaf pen' by choosing an out-of-the-way corner of the garden, knocking four posts into the ground in a square, and stretching wire netting around them. Fill the pen with fallen leaves, and put an old piece of carpet over the top to stop them blowing away. The only thing is that they take about a year to rot sufficiently for you to use the mixture.

Tidy up borders: By this time most herbaceous plants will have lost most of their leaves and many will have died down to practically nothing. Cut off all remaining dead and dying stems and leaves (but make sure you leave the green leaves and stems of *Helleborus*).

Prepare the soil: New beds may be dug, and old ones renovated (see Early Winter).

Check supports: Supports for trees and climbing plants growing on trelliswork should always be firm, but the action of autumn frosts and winds, or simple old age can cause them to be broken or otherwise unstable. Now is a good time to replace these where necessary. Also, check that ties are secure on the trees, without being too tight.

SECTION TWO

LEFT **Many decorative hardy plants are suitable for growing in acidic soil. This is pasque flower, which prefers soils in the pH 5.0–6.0 range.**

**TYPICAL PLANT
HARDINESS ZONES
FOR WESTERN EUROPE**

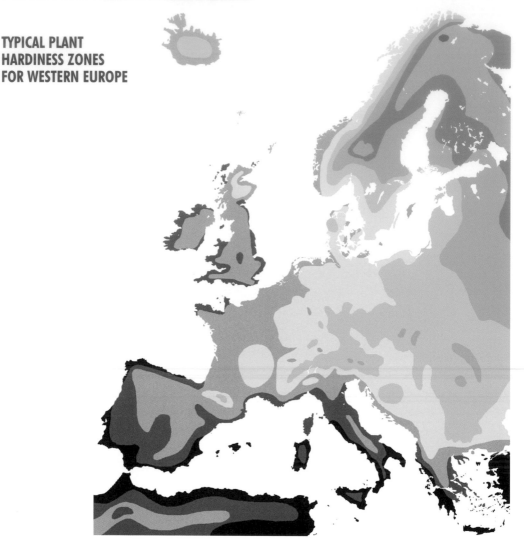

When one talks of plants growing on an acid soil one immediately thinks of rhododendrons. These are essentially woodland plants and many of them originated in the warm, humid forests of Asia. However, heathers are just as famous for their preference for acid soil, yet these are tough little customers and many naturally grow on bleak, open Scottish moorlands.

It is clear, therefore, that acid-loving plants can come from an extreme range of conditions. Some of them thrive in very hot places, whilst others need a cool climate. It is worth remembering, also, that new plants are being developed all the time, and often it is hardiness,

and other weather tolerances, that is being bred into them. It is useful to know, therefore, when buying your plants, which climate suits them best and the parts of the world in which they originated usually dictate this.

If you live in Europe or the US, the maps on these pages will give you an indication of the plant hardiness zones for where you live.

However, as you will see from the Directory section that follows, plants for acid soils can be adaptable, so – wherever you live – it should be possible to find a selection of good plants that will suit the requirements of both you and your garden.

TYPICAL PLANT HARDINESS ZONES FOR NORTH AMERICA

Keys to colours (both maps)

⬤	Zone 1	below −50°F (−46°C)
⬤	Zone 2	−50 to −40°F (−46 to −40°C)
⬤	Zone 3	−40 to −30°F (−40 to −34.5°C)
⬤	Zone 4	−30 to −20°F (−34 to −29°C)
⬤	Zone 5	−20 to −10°F (−29 to −23°C)
⬤	Zone 6	−10 to 0°F (−23 to −18°C)
⬤	Zone 7	0 to 10°F (−18 to −12°C)
⬤	Zone 8	10 to 20°F (−12 to −7°C)
⬤	Zone 9	20 to 30°F (−7 to −1°C)
⬤	Zone 10	30 to 40°F (−1 to 4°C)
⬤	Zone 11	above 40°F (above 4°C)

HOW TO USE THESE MAPS

Each entry in the plant directory lists the relevant zones where it should be possible to grow the plant successfully, based on these heat-zone maps. Find your location on the map, and you can then identify the zone that your area belongs to. Do not forget to take into account that cities are warmer than rural locations. Planting shelter belts of trees, even if these are in the shade and/or in raised, well-drained beds, can help to give plants better conditions in which to thrive.

CHAPTER 7

A–Z Plant Directory

This part of the book will be an invaluable source of reference when you are choosing plants for your acid soil. Listed here are many of our most popular garden plants for such situations, which are listed alphabetically – by Latin name – within the section that relates to their type (annuals, bulbs, perennials, trees and shrubs, and so on). Under each of the descriptions are these items of information:

Origin: This tells you, if known, where the species was discovered. Understanding where a plant comes from, the country or part of the world, with its average climate or even altitude, can help you to understand its growing requirements and conditions.

Type: The 'type' of plant – for example, whether it is grown from a bulb as opposed to a tuber, corm or rhizome, or whether it is an annual (grows, flowers and dies within one year) or a biennial (the same but in two years), or perhaps a shrub rather than a climber.

AWARD OF GARDEN MERIT

Throughout this A–Z Directory you will see the initials AGM set after certain plants. This denotes that the plant in question has passed certain assessments carried out by experts under the auspices of the Royal Horticultural Society in Great Britain. Only plants with exceptionally good garden qualities can be awarded this special Award of Garden Merit.

USDA zone: These are the climate zones referred to on pages 78 and 79, designed to identify the relative hardiness of plants. The zone numbers quoted here, based on UK Royal Horticultural Society data, are on the cautious side, so if you are not prepared to take any chances, follow the hardiness ratings to the letter. Otherwise there is a great deal of leeway. Raised beds, good drainage, tree cover, east-facing as opposed to west-facing gardens, and planting against a house wall all give plants a better habitat – so be prepared to experiment.

Preferred pH range: The plants included in this Directory are likely to thrive if the soil in which they are growing is between the range of pH points given. This is the optimum acidity level for the particular plant. However, if your soil is higher or lower than the pH range in question it does not necessarily mean that your plants will die, nor that the situation is impossible to rectify. The pH can be made higher or lower accordingly, by following the processes discussed on pages 22–25.

Description: Here you will discover generalized details of the plant's shape, size and demeanour, along with flower and foliage colour and shape.

Popular species and varieties: A plant species may exist without offspring or siblings, so will have a relatively small entry in this book. But with, for example, the *Erica* (heather) genus, there are many different species and cultivars (abbreviation of 'cultivated variety') and so there will be many to recommend.

ANNUALS, BIENNIALS AND BEDDING PLANTS

NAME: AMARANTHUS CAUDATUS (LOVE-LIES-BLEEDING)

Origin: Peru, Africa, India
Type: Hardy annual
USDA Zone: Z5
Preferred pH range: 6.0–6.5
Description: This annual is unmistakable, with its long flowers spikes, which may be erect and up-standing, or trailing and hanging vertically, depending on variety. These plants usually flower for a long period in summer. Sow seed in early spring in the flowering position; it likes a well-drained, reasonably fertile soil in a warm, sunny position. Thin out seedlings to 9–12in (23–30cm) apart. Plants have a height of up to 3ft (90cm).

Popular species and varieties: *Amaranthus paniculatus* (also known as *A. cruentus*) has several excellent cultivars, of which 'Foxtail' has upward-pointing spikes of deep red, and 'Autumn Palette', similar but in shades of cream and biscuit. *A. caudatus* 'Crimson' has long, crimson-pink, drooping tassels and light green foliage; 'Ribbons and Beads' has vibrant red and green tassels. *A. tricolor* 'Early Splendour' is grown for its beautiful foliage; the large rosy red leaves turn a deep chocolate-brown as they age.

NAME: ANTIRRHINUM MAJUS (SNAPDRAGON)

Origin: Man-made hybrids from parent plants originating throughout the temperate parts of the world
Type: Tender perennial grown as an annual
USDA Zone: Z7
Preferred pH range: 5.5–7.0
Description: This is a very versatile summer-flowering bedding plant, that can be grown in various garden situations, being excellent as a border filler, bed edging, or as a container plant. The common name derives from its flower, which opens like a mouth when squeezed.

ABOVE *Amaranthus paniculatus* 'Foxtail'

81

ABOVE *Antirrhinum* 'Pearly Queen Mixed'

Plants that are not removed from the garden in autumn will usually survive in winter (provided it is not too harsh), and they will flower again for a second year; the best flowers, however, are always on young, or first-year plants. Tall-growing varieties can be used as cut flowers in the home. Dwarf types are best used as main bedding or edging plants.

Popular species and varieties There are dozens of varieties ranging in height from 6–36in (15–90cm). The Axiom Series produces tall flower spikes in seven colours, and is recommended for adding height to borders. Trailing types, such as 'Luminaire' and 'Pearly Queen Mixed', are good for using in hanging baskets and containers. 'Tequila Sunrise' is a blend of varieties, all with bronze foliage and bright, cherry flowers in orange, red and yellow. 'Frosted Flames' is an intriguing mixture, as the leaves appear to have a 'frosting' over them.

NAME: *BACOPA/SUTERA*

Origin: South Africa
Type: Annual
USDA Zone: Z7–9
Preferred pH range: 5.5–6.0
Description: Rarely is there a plant with such variation – and confusion – over its correct botanical and commercial naming. *Sutera* is more often than not referred to as *Bacopa*, most nurseryman recognizing this name. However botanically the true *Bacopa* is a separate but related genus (both plants being in the snapdragon family, *Scrophulariaceae*). To further confuse, the Scopia™ strain is often seen under Copia®; forms of *Sutera cordata* are sometimes listed as *Suteranova*, and the form known as the 'yellow *Bacopa*' is actually *Mecardonia*, an entirely new genus. Regardless of the name confusion, these are all popular hanging basket and container plants because of

ABOVE *Bacopa Scopia*™ Gulliver White

their delicate flowers, which come in profusion, and the plants' rampant growth. This is a tender plant that has only been available widely within the past decade, although the white form 'Snowflake' is much older.

Foliage is small and mid-green, and plants generally have a creeping habit. The flowers have five petals, and they are produced in quantity all summer. If planted into borders, a single plant can cover an area 2sq ft (60cm²). When planted in a hanging basket, windowbox or other container it will cascade over the sides to form a sheet of flowers and foliage at least 12in (30cm) long. Growth is so dense that it sometimes crowds out weaker plants, such as busy Lizzies, so it needs room to grow.

Popular species and varieties: The first forms commonly available were white, but pink and blue varieties are now widespread. It has to be said that the differences between the various colours and strains are small, and it takes a real expert to identify them. It is surprising therefore that so much energy has gone into breeding and development work. The truth is that because the volume of sales is so large, even a small percentage increase through the introduction of a new strain can reap huge rewards for the breeder. *Bacopa* 'Cabana White' has long, spreading stems bearing white flowers in summer to early autumn.

'Snowflake' is much older. There are also trailing blue and lavender forms with the Cabana pre-fix. *B. Scopia*™ Gulliver White is one of the top-selling forms; white flowers; vigorous. *B. Scopia*™ Pink Touch has large, light pink blooms with purple markings; flowers from early summer. *S. cordata* 'Snowflake' is the original *Sutera/Bacopa* emerging from the wilds of South Africa; a mass of small white flowers are carried on green, trailing foliage.

83

ABOVE *Calendula* 'Daisy Mixed'

NAME: *CALENDULA* (POT MARIGOLD)

Origin: Mediterranean region
Type: Hardy annual
USDA Zone: Z6–9
Preferred pH range: 5.5–7.0
Description: A cottage garden favourite, this hardy annual may be sown in autumn for overwintering and flowering the following summer. It is called 'marigold' for its flowers resemble the typical hybrid marigold flowers of the *Tagetes* genus. But plants are distinguishable in that *Calendula* leaves are oval, and slightly hairy, whereas *Tagetes* leaves are usually a darker green, and are segmented or divided. I have found that calendulas are, to a certain extent, immune to slug and snail damage (probably due to the hirsute nature of the foliage), unlike *Tagetes*, which is an absolute favourite of the gastropods.
Popular species and varieties: *Calendula officinalis* is the commonly grown species, with bright orange, single flowers. The following cultivars are well worth growing: 'Art Shades Mixed' (shades of apricot, orange and cream), 'Greenheart Orange' (rich orange and lime green) and 'Daisy Mixed' (golden yellow, orange and cream).

ABOVE *Celosia* 'Century Fire'

NAME: *CELOSIA ARGENTEA* (COCKSCOMB)

Origin: Tropical and sub-tropical Asia, Africa and America
Type: Hardy annual
USDA Zone: Z9
Preferred pH range: 6.0–7.0
Description: The *Celosia* makes a fine specimen pot plant for a greenhouse or conservatory, but it may also be used in bedding schemes when planted in quantity. The flowers come in dense plumes, giving rise to an alternative common name of Prince of Wales' feathers.
Popular species and varieties: *Celosia argentea* is divided into two groups: the Cristata types, which have crested flowers and make better pot plants (if they are bedded out and the summer is wet, water can rest in the flattened flowerheads, causing them to rot),

and the Plumosa types, which are best for bedding out. The Plumosa Century Series, of which 'Century Fire' is one of the most vibrant-coloured forms, is the best for bedding. *C. spicata* has slender flower spikes and can be used as cut flowers; to my mind the best form is 'Flamingo Feather', with pinkish flowers.

NAME: *CLARKIA ELEGANS* (Syn. *C. UNGUICULARIS*)

Origin: California
Type: Hardy annual
USDA Zone: Z9
Preferred pH range: 6.0–6.5
Description: Often sold under its newer name of *Clarkia unguicularis*, this hardy annual flowers

all through the summer, and thrives best in a light, well-drained soil and in full sunshine. Sow as soon as the soil is ready in the spring and perhaps once or twice later if flowers for cutting are desired for longer periods. Thin out seedlings to 12in (30cm) apart.

The eventual height is around 2ft (60cm); support plants with brushwood before they become too tall, since *Clarkia* is apt to snap off at soil level.

Popular species and varieties: Mostly mixtures of bright shades of red, white, pink and mauve are available, such as 'Choice Double Mixed'. One exceptionally good cultivar is 'Apple Blossom', with masses of fully double blooms in soft apricot pink with a hint of white.

ABOVE *Clarkia elegans*

ABOVE *Coreopsis tinctoria* 'Mahogany Midget'

NAME: *COREOPSIS* (TICKSEED)

Origin: North and South America
Type: Tender perennial mainly grown as an annual
USDA Zone: Z4–5
Preferred pH range: 5.0–6.0
Description: These are easy-to-grow perennials that flower in the first year from seed. They are, therefore, frequently grown as annuals, and discarded after one year. There are several varieties, all of which are notable for their bright daisy flowers. To some they are vulgar, but it is largely a matter of placing. They are free-flowering plants, good for a sunny border, and all are good for cutting and bringing indoors.
Popular species and varieties: *Coreopsis tinctoria* 'Mahogany Midget' is one of the deepest coloured, and blooms throughout summer and early autumn. *C. verticillata* is extremely floriferous and may be found in shades of yellow; it grows to around 2ft (60cm). The cultivar 'Zagreb' AGM is a very uniform golden yellow. 'Goldfink' is only about 1ft (30cm) and flowers over a long period, whilst *C. grandiflora* 'Mayfield Giant' and 'Rising Sun' are tall varieties, up to 3ft (90cm).

NAME: *GAZANIA* (TREASURE FLOWER)

Origin: Tropical and Southern Africa
Type: Tender annual
USDA Zone: Z9
Preferred pH range: 5.5–7.0
Description: On a bright and sunny summer's day there is little that can surpass the *Gazania* for brilliance. But if the day is cloudy or wet,

ABOVE *Gazania* 'Daybreak Bronze'

most of the flowers remain closed for protection, and the border can therefore be dull. This is the main reason these plants are not as popular as they should be. The good news is that breeders have bred modern varieties, and they seem increasingly to keep their flowers open in cloudy weather, so they are at least worth a try for the masses. The daisy-shaped flowers are invariably deep yellow to orange, but they have various markings which give the *Gazania* its edge over other plants. Many have olive green or black zones, whilst others have brown or red stripes.

There are brick-red, mahogany and cream variations, too. Plants reach 8–10in (20–25cm) in height.

Popular species and varieties: The 'Daybreak Series' is reliable, has a good colour range (including yellow, orange, deep orange and bronze), and is one of the modern varieties that flower in dull weather. The 'Kiss Series' is known for the darker, central zones to its otherwise bright flowers. 'Tiger Mixture' has large, vibrant flowers that are striped variously white, orange and yellow.

ABOVE *Helichrysum petiolatum* 'Dargon Hill Monarch'

ABOVE *Impatiens* 'Escapade'

NAME: *HELICHRYSUM* (EVERLASTING FLOWER)

Origin: South Africa, Australia
Type: Tender perennial which is best treated as an annual
USDA Zone: Z7–10
Preferred pH range: 5.0–6.0
Description: This is a large genus of perennials some of which are woody, and therefore classed as sub-shrubs. A few types are best grown as annuals, with fresh seed being sown every year. The most colourful form is *Helichrysum monstrosum*, which is known variously as everlasting flower or straw flower. Bright, rounded daisy heads in rich colours are carried on stems 15–36in (38–90cm) high.

When cut and brought indoors the flowers retain their shape and colour for months; the drying out process does not seem to weaken or degrade them significantly.
Popular species and varieties: *Helichrysum monstrosum* 'Bright Bikini Mixed' produces flowers in a wide range of bright, warm colours on stems 15in (38cm) high. 'Summer Solstice' is similar on taller plants at 36in (90cm).

NAME: *IMPATIENS* (BUSY LIZZIE)

Origin: Globally, except South America, Australia and New Zealand
Type: Tender perennial, designed to be grown as an annual

USDA Zone: 10

Preferred pH range: 5.5–6.5

Description: These are low-growing summer bedding plants known for their free-flowering nature. They come in a variety of colours from white and pale pink through to oranges, deep reds and near purple. Yellow and blue shades have yet to be bred. All flower from early summer until the autumn frosts. Usefully, they grow well if planted in a border that receives light shade – a position where many others would fail.

Popular species and varieties: 'Super Elfin' series of F1 hybrids, to 10in (25cm), available in individual colours, such as 'Lipstick' (rose-pink), 'Salmon Blush' (peachy salmon) and 'Velvet Red' (deep red), or 'Fiesta Sparkling Rose', or a mixture, as in 'Bruno' F1 hybrid, with large flowers up to 2½in (6cm) across, growing to 9in (23cm). The 'Accent Bright Eye' Series has flowers of more than 2in (5cm) across. The Spellbound range, including 'Cranberry Cauldron' and 'Fairy Pink', are particularly free-flowering. The New Guinea Hybrids are a strain with much larger leaves. They arguably make better specimen plants for growing in pots and containers than for bedding, although they can be very successful when planted out into borders. 'Escapade' is a particularly eye-catching New Guinea type with scarlet flowers.

NAME: *MYOSOTIS SYLVATICA* (FORGET-ME-NOT)

Origin: Throughout Europe and parts of Asia

Type: Biennial

USDA Zone: Z4–8

Preferred pH range: 6.0–7.0

Description: Spring gardens in temperate parts of the world come alive with these low-growing, moisture-loving plants. They are prized for their small but numerous – usually blue – flowers. In the self-sown forms there will be some flowers with a central white eye, and others with a yellow eye. Forget-me-nots prefer a moist soil, cool weather and, curiously, they like crowded

ABOVE *Myosotis sylvatica*

conditions where they can support each other in a border. They are particularly good as a planting beneath and between taller bulbs, such as tulips and crown imperials.

Popular species and varieties: The flowers of 'Bobo Mixed' are normally blue, but pink and white blooms also appear on different plants; 'Royal Blue Improved' is taller, at 12in (30cm), and has deep indigo-blue flowers. 'Blue Ball' produces compact, ball-shaped plants just 6in (15cm) tall, with flowers of bright blue.

ABOVE *Nicotiana* 'Tinkerbell'

NAME: *NICOTIANA ALATA* (FLOWERING TOBACCO PLANT)

Origin: South America
Type: Annual or short-lived perennial
USDA Zone: Z7
Preferred pH range: 5.5–6.5
Description: Nicotianas are popular garden plants for their showy flowers which first open at night. Each flower lasts for a long time before it drops. The sap of the plant has narcotic and poisonous properties, which is hardly surprising when you come to realize that tobacco is derived from the close relative, *Nicotiana tabacum*. The garden annuals recommended here can reach 5ft (1.5m) in height, with branching stems. The blooms are frequently fragrant, and are shaped like small trumpets or funnels. Colours are numerous, including white, pink, mauve, red, maroon, purple and even pale green. Plants usually set seed readily and a crop of plants for flowering the following year can be the result – but do not rely on the colours as most of them will be different to those of the parent plants.

Popular species and varieties: *Nicotiana sylvestris* produces a candelabra of highly fragrant white blooms – a choice plant for the border, or as a 'dot' plant amongst other bedding, and a real talking point. Many more colourful varieties are available, some with relatively large flowers; then some of the dwarf kinds have even showier but less fragrant blooms. 'Domino Antique Shades' is a hybrid strain with a compact habit just 12in (30cm) high, making it perfect for pots and border edges; 'Tinkerbell', at 36in (90cm) high, has dusky rose-pink flowers with contrasting lime-green backs, and blue pollen. *Nicotiana knightiana* 'Green Tears' is smothered in small, two-toned green, teardrop-like blooms.

ABOVE *Ricinis communis*

NAME: *RICINUS* (CASTOR OIL PLANT)

Origin: Throughout the sub-tropical world
Type: Tender annual
USDA Zone: Z9
Preferred pH range: 5.5–6.5
Description: This is a popular foliage plant for the summer, and it makes a very good 'dot' plant in a carpet of low-growing bedding plants. In frost-free areas it forms a large, spreading shrub, but as a bedding plant it will normally grow to just 4ft (1.2m) or so. Its leaves are large and boldly lobed. Although the wild species has green leaves, most garden varieties have foliage flushed with maroon or bronze tints. The flowers are insignificant, but they are followed by showy, prickly seedpods that are often brightly coloured. These pods each contain three large seeds (which are poisonous – the derivative of the poison ricin).
Popular species and varieties: *Ricinis communis* 'Carmencita' has dark brown foliage with red flowers and fruit; 'Carmencita Pink' has green leaves and reddish stalks; 'Impala' produces large bronze leaves, which are maroon when young, and red fruits.

ABOVE *Tagetes* 'Queen Sofia'

NAME: *TAGETES* (MARIGOLD)

Origin: Man-made hybrids from parent plants originating in tropical Mexico and Central America

Type: Half hardy annual

USDA Zone: Z9

Preferred pH range: 5.5–7.0

Description: There are French (*Tagetes patula*) and African marigolds (*T. erecta*), and they both come originally from Central America. The leaves are dark green, and have toothed margins. They are attractive, but have a pungent aroma, which is frequently disliked – except by slugs, which adore them.

Popular species and varieties: African marigold cultivars range from 8–20in (20–50cm) in height, with flowerheads up to 4in (10cm) across. The cultivars are all double-flowered. Dwarf cultivars are often top heavy, needing a spacious setting if they are not to look incongruous. They come in shades of yellow, cream and orange. 'Vanilla' has attractive, cream-coloured flowers. In French marigolds, red and mahogany shades are common. Cultivars range from 6–12in (15–30cm) in height, with flowerheads up to 2½in (6cm) across. Many cultivars are in shades of red and mahogany, most commonly in bi-colour combinations with yellow. 'Queen Sophia' has red flowers becoming bronze with maturity, each petal edged with gold. The Espana and Bonanza Series are both highly regarded, noted for their earliness, uniformity and reliability under a wide range of conditions. The Afro-French marigolds are hybrids between *T. erecta* and *T. patula*. *Tagetes tenuifolia* is an attractive mound-forming annual with masses of small yellow flowers and highly pungent foliage when brushed with the hand.

NAME: *VIOLA* (PANSY)

Origin: Throughout temperate parts of the world
Type: Short-lived perennials best grown as annuals
USDA Zone: Z6–10
Preferred pH range: 5.5–7.0
Description: All pansies are violas, but not all violas are pansies! Some forms of *Viola*, such as *V. odorata* or the cultivar 'Tiger Eye', are regarded as 'violas', with smallish and usually more numerous blooms. The larger-flowered hybrids are generally referred to as pansies. Both types, however, are hardy, short-lived perennials that are best grown as annuals or biennials. A huge range of colours is available, from singles with no markings to others that are heavily blotched and several colours fading in to each other. The winter-flowering types have been bred to flower during the cold, short days of winter, but even with these plants the best blooms are carried in late winter and early spring when average temperatures are slightly higher. Then there are those types that are summer-flowering, and then will carry on through most of autumn. Some of the best pansy displays come in planting yellows and purples (of any variety) together.

Popular species and varieties: Of the summer-flowering pansies, 'Singing The Blues' is a mixture of four different blue shades; plants have a trailing tendency, and the blooms have a sweet scent. 'Universal' is the name given to the best strain of winter-flowering pansy; uniform habit with mixed colours in flowers of medium size. *Viola cornuta* 'Valentine' is a lovely hybrid producing flowers in a combination of rosy-pink and white, with a blushed primrose-yellow eye.

ABOVE **Mixed spring-flowering pansies in yellow and purple contrast well.**

ANNUALS AND BIENNIALS PREFERRING SOILS IN THE NEUTRAL RANGE

The following plants thrive in a soil with a pH range that straddles both the higher levels of acidity and the lower levels of alkalinity

Latin name	Common name	pH range
Ageratum	Floss flower	6.0–7.5
Althaea	Hollyhock	6.0–7.5
Alyssum	Madwort/Alyssum	6.0–7.5
Anchusa	Bugloss/Alkanet	6.0–7.5
Armeria	Thrift	6.0–7.5
Aster	Starwort/Daisy plant/Michaelmas daisy	5.5–7.5
Calceolaria	Slipper flower	6.0–7.5
Campanula	Canterbury bells	6.0–7.5
Centaurea	Cornflower/Knapweed	5.5–7.5
Dianthus	Annual carnation/Sweet William	6.5–8.5
Digitalis	Foxglove	6.0–7.5
Erysimum	Wallflower	5.5–7.5
Gaillardia	Blanket flower	6.0–7.5
Godetia	Farewell-to-spring	6.0–7.5
Gypsophila	Baby's breath	6.0–7.5
Helianthus	Sunflower	6.0–7.5
Iberis	Candytuft	6.0–7.5
Ipomoea	Morning glory	6.0–7.5
Lobelia	Lobelia	6.0–7.5
Leucanthemum	Marguerite	6.0–7.5
Lathyrus	Sweet pea	6.0–7.5
Matthiola	Stock	6.0–7.5
Nasturtium	Nasturtium	5.5–7.5
Papaver	Poppy	6.0–7.5
Petunia	Petunia	6.0–7.5
Portulaca	Sun plant/Ross moss	5.5–8.0
Pyrethrum	Pyrethrum	6.0–7.5
Salvia	Salvia/Sage	6.0–7.5
Scabiosa	Scabious	5.0–8.0
Zinnia	Zinnia/Youth-and-old-age	5.5–8.0

ABOVE Aster 'Compliment'

ABOVE Pink flowered biennial Canterbury bell
(*Campanula media* 'Chelsea Pink')

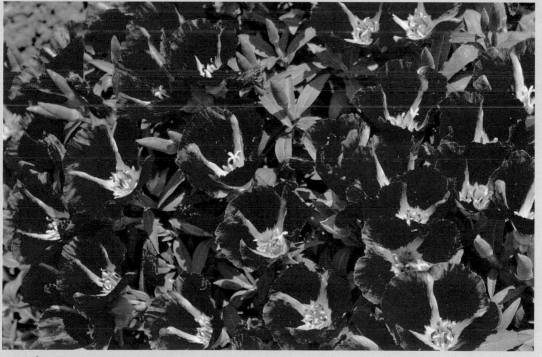

ABOVE Godetia Satin 'Deep Rose'

BULBS

NAME: *ANEMONE* (WINDFLOWER)

Origin: Worldwide

Type: Tuberous perennials

USDA Zone: Z5–8

Preferred pH range: 4.5–6.5

Description: There are perennial anemones, such as *Anemone* x *hybrida*, and those that grow from tubers, which are included here. The dwarf *A. blanda* produces blue, pink or white daisy-like flowers in spring. It is excellent for growing among shrubs in a border, or for naturalizing in a woodland garden. The well-known *A. coronaria*, also from tubers, is ideal for the border and flowers a few weeks later; this species produces red, white or blue flowers, good for cutting and bringing indoors. They tolerate a lightly shaded spot, but are usually far happier in full sun. The aforementioned *Anemone* x *hybrida*, and other autumn-flowering fibrous-rooted forms, are happiest in light shade and prefer alkaline soils.

Popular species and varieties: *Anemone blanda* AGM grows to just 6in (15cm) in height; it has open daisy-like flowers, the first of which, in mild seasons, can appear even in mid-winter. Frequently sold in a mixture, it is worth searching for the few named varieties available, including 'Radar' AGM (a striking bright magenta with a white eye); 'White Splendour' (large, pure white flowers); and 'Charmer' (a clear pink). *Anemone coronaria* is mainly grown in one of two strains – the De Caen (sometimes referred to as the poppy anemone) and St Brigid mixtures. Colours for both forms range from deep blue and purple, through to red, pink and white. The St Brigids also come in semi-double or double-flowering forms. Several named varieties are available, including the single 'Hollandia' (scarlet), the double 'Lord Lieutenant' (blue), the double 'Sylphide' (magenta) and single 'The Bride' (pure white).

ABOVE *Anemone coronaria* 'Lord Lieutenant'

ABOVE *Begonia* 'Finale Orange'

NAME: *BEGONIA*

Origin: Worldwide
Type: Tuberous perennials
USDA Zone: Z10
Preferred pH range: 5.5–6.5
Description: There are some begonias that are grown as annuals (including *Begonia semperflorens*, popular as summer bedding plants). These enjoy a neutral soil. However, the tuberous kinds with big, blousy flowers are rather more acid-loving. These plants are great favourites for providing summer colour, with the large-flowered varieties being excellent for pots in the conservatory, windowboxes or patio containers. They can also be used for bedding out but not before all danger of frost has passed. The pendulous varieties are excellent for growing in hanging baskets. Tuberous begonias are not hardy, so they should not be planted outside before late spring. Some of the tuberous types are referred to as the 'pendulous begonias', as they produce long, soft stems that trail over the sides of pots and hanging baskets. There are many *Begonia* flower forms – single, double, some with heavily ruffled petals, also camellia- and carnation-flowered varieties (often listed as *B.* x *tuberhybrida*).

Popular species and varieties: Among the most popular forms are 'Bouton de Rose' with double well-formed blooms of pink edged with white, and 'Marmorata', its carmine flowers are marbled with white, and the petals of which are ruffled and waved. The graceful pendulous begonias produce a large number of flowers over a long period; one of the best is the richly coloured 'Finale Orange'.

ABOVE *Colchicum speciosum* **'Atrorubens'**

NAME: *COLCHICUM AUTUMNALE* (AUTUMN CROCUS)

Origin: Central and Western Europe
Type: Perennial corm
USDA Zone: Z5
Preferred pH range: 5.5–6.5
Description: Colchicums produce flowers that look very similar to the spring-flowering *Crocus*, and for this reason they are referred to as 'autumn crocus'. In reality, however, they are not related to each other at all. Colchicums emerge from the soil in late summer, as just flower buds – the foliage does not show itself until late winter. When in full leaf, colchicums are large, and have been known to smother smaller plants. Two words of warning: they are poisonous, and they can look unsightly in a border when dying back, so choose their position carefully.

Popular species and varieties: The most commonly seen species is *Colchicum autumnale*, which produces masses of lilac-pink goblet-shaped flowers – and all from a single corm. It is a good plant for naturalizing in grass. 'Alboplenum' is white, double and produces three to five flowers from each bulb. 'The Giant' has rose-lilac flowers on 10in (25cm) long stalks; each flower has a white base. If you prefer something a little less showy, there is the single, white cultivar, 'Album'. *C. speciosum* 'Waterlily' AGM has purplish-lilac double flowers, and in many ways does resemble a waterlily bloom. 'Atrorubens' is, to my mind, a more pleasing plant, with vivid sugar-pink petals. 'Lilac Wonder', in my experience, seems to be more vigorous and more hardy than any of the others; its flowers are deep lilac-pink.

ABOVE *Cyclamen hederifolium* AGM

NAME: *CYCLAMEN*

Origin: Southern Europe and the Mediterranean
Type: Tuberous perennials
USDA Zone: Z6–9
Preferred pH range: 6.0–7.0
Description: Perhaps best known as the winter-flowering pot plant, the *Cyclamen* genus is for bringing into conservatories and cool rooms in the home. The hardy forms, however, are highly effective when grown en masse and in time they will grow into large colonies of colour. They are particularly useful for growing in shady spots under trees.

Popular species and varieties: *C. hederifolium* AGM comes into bloom in late summer; the first flowers often appear just after rainfall. There are both pink and white forms. The leaves tend to open much later, just as the flowers are going over, and the shapes and patterning – marbling, blotching and silvering – on the leaves vary greatly. Late winter will see the pointed buds of *C. coum* AGM open to pink or white flowers. Leaves are usually rounded with silver and green patterning on the top surface, and plain dark red on the underside. Although the plants themselves are tough, the leaves may be damaged by severe frost. Other *Cyclamen* of note include *C. libanoticum* AGM, with large clear pink flowers in spring; *C. repandum*, having beautifully reddish-purple turned-back petals in spring; *C. cilicium* AGM produces pink flowers in autumn; *C. cilicium* f. *album* has white autumn flowers; and *C. graecum*, has pink flowers that are held well clear of the heavily marbled leaves in late autumn and early winter.

ABOVE *Gladiolus* 'Deciso'

NAME: *GLADIOLUS* (SWORD LILY)

Origin: Africa (mainly South Africa), Madagascar, Arabia, Europe, Western Asia

Type: Perennial corm

USDA Zone: Z9

Preferred pH range: 6.0–7.0

Description: Modern garden *Gladiolus* hybrids come in a wide spectrum of colours but beware: most are not hardy, so in most temperate regions the corms need to be lifted in the autumn and replanted the following spring. The exceptions are the Nanus gladioli (see below). Plant corms of all types in a sunny place in good, humus-rich, well-drained soil. Plant in spring 3–4in (7.5–10cm) deep and 6in (15cm) apart. Stagger planting between early and late spring to give a succession of blooms. These are not universally popular garden plants today, many gardeners preferring to grow them instead in rows in the kitchen garden, or on a spare piece of ground, to provide cut flowers for indoors. Individual plants do require staking, and this contributes to their being difficult as border garden plants, or less appealing to the eye as container plants.

Popular species and varieties: Among the many large-flowered hybrids are: 'Nova Lux', a primrose yellow, 'Applause', a carmine-rose, and 'Traderhorn', a scarlet with ivory-white flecks. Butterfly gladiolus are smaller flowered, growing up to 36in (90cm), and are widely used in floral arrangements. Many of the florets are ruffled or frilled. 'Liebelei' is an eye-catching scarlet with a cream throat, 'Silver Shadow' is a delicate pink fading to white and 'Spring Green' is a striking lime green. *Gladiolus communis* subsp. *byzantinus* AGM is a plant from Mediterranean regions; its flower spike can be 24in (60cm) high, with loosely arranged wine-red florets. In many mild districts it can be left in the ground undisturbed. Similarly the Nanus types are hardier than the large-flowered hybrids. Look for: 'Albus' (white), 'Carine' (ivory with cerise flecks) and 'Mirella' (vibrant orange). There are dozens of other varieties and cultivars available and it is recommended that you consult a specialist's catalogue before you make your choice.

NAME: *IRIS* (BULBOUS)

There are two main types of iris – those growing from bulbs, and others grown from rhizomes. Let's consider the bulbous forms first.

Type: Bulbous perennials

Origin: Temperate regions of the northern hemisphere

USDA Zone: Z5–10

Preferred pH range: 5.0–6.5

Description: The bulbous irises comprise a large group of species, but only a handful are grown by gardeners; the vast majority are considered

ABOVE *Iris reticulata 'Pauline'*

choice plants only really admired by specialist enthusiasts and alpine garden hobbyists. The more familiar species include the miniature bulbs such as *Iris danfordiae* and *I. reticulata*. These smaller bulbs are generally grown on rock or scree gardens, or confined to pots in an unheated greenhouse (which could loosely be termed an 'alpine house'). The first of them will bloom in late winter and early spring, especially if the winter is a mild one, and they are often to be seen in flower at the same time as crocuses. Then there are taller Dutch irises whose flowers are particularly good for cutting. These can be grown in mixed borders, or in rows on the vegetable plot, making them easier to cut.

Popular species and varieties: *Iris danfordiae* has lovely deep yellow flowers with green spots in the throat. *I. histrioides* 'Major' AGM has rich blue flowers just 6in (15cm) high. *I. reticulata* AGM has deep mauve flowers highlighted by gold markings on the falls. Named varieties include 'Harmony' (sky blue and royal blue, with yellow-rimmed white blotches), 'Pauline' (dusky violet-pink highlighted by a large white spot on the falls) and 'Katherine Hodgkin' AGM (large pale blue flowers with yellow markings). Of the Dutch irises look out for: 'Bronze Beauty' (bronze-orange), 'Eye of the Tiger' (deep purple with a yellow blotch) and 'Rusty Beauty' (orange standards with falls of a deeper orange).

ABOVE *Iris unguicularis* **'Bob Thompson'**

NAME: *IRIS* (RHIZOMATOUS)

Type: Rhizomatous irises
Origin: Temperate regions of the northern hemisphere
USDA Zone: Z5–10
Preferred pH range: 5.0–6.5
Description: Most gardeners know the tall bearded irises with their stiff sword-shaped foliage, and it is the hybrid forms that are grown mainly. The range of colours and combinations is huge, so it is best to study the catalogue of a specialist in *Iris*, or look for them in springtime at a garden centre. Easy-to-grow, the rhizomes are planted so the top is showing above the ground.

Popular species and varieties: *Iris germanica* AGM is often referred to as purple flag, or London flag. In late spring and early summer it produces scented blooms with rich purple falls and a white beard; the standards are of light purple. It grows to between 24–36in (60–90cm), depending on the variety.

The dwarf bearded irises are excellent for the front of a border or sunny pocket in the rock garden. Their heights range from 4–12in (10–30cm). They are fully hardy and are again available in a wide range of colours. 'Lacy Snowflake' is one of the brightest, purest white flowers. A semi-dwarf bearded iris is 'Blue Denim', with lovely mauve-blue flowers.

Flowering in the depths of winter is the Algerian iris, *I. unguicularis* (AGM). Varieties to look out for are 'Bob Thompson' and 'Palette' – the latter, as its name indicates, comprises a mixture of several colours.

In addition to the 'dry soil' rhizomatous irises, there are several species suitable for bog gardens, traditionally places with soils of a very acidic nature. The best known is the yellow flag, *I. pseudacorus* AGM. This is one for the edge of a large pond or lake; clumps grow too large for smaller gardens. It will grow happily in shallow water. The Siberian iris, *I. sibirica* AGM requires a good, moist soil; it will not grow in waterlogged conditions. It reaches around 36in (90cm) and has long narrow leaves, with the flowers held well clear of the foliage on strong stems. There are a considerable number of named varieties, many with blue flowers, together with white and yellow. One of the most impressive moisture lovers is the summer-flowering Japanese iris, *I. ensata* AGM. The flat flowers can be up to 8in (20cm) across, single or double, single coloured, or blended or netted with different coloured veining. There are dozens of named varieties, but one that stands out is 'Rowden Autocrat', a very pale blue with dark blue veining and yellow markings.

ABOVE *Lilium* 'Arena'

NAME: *LILIUM* (LILY)

Origin: Throughout the temperate regions of the northern hemisphere
Type: Bulbous perennials
USDA Zone: Z4–7
Preferred pH range: 6.0–7.0
Description: Lilies are incredibly popular, and garden centres tend to stock many varieties. These are, however, a drop in the ocean, as there are hundreds listed in specialist catalogues, many varieties being quite rare.

Lilies are quite happy in the ground provided they are not too exposed, are not in full sun, and have a soil that is constantly damp but never waterlogged. They also make perfect plants for large pots, for bringing into full view when they are in flower. Flowers vary from outward-facing, to trumpet-shaped flattish blooms, and some referred to as Turk's cap lilies, with nodding, downward-facing flowers. Many lilies are fragrant, so these should be positioned somewhere where they can be enjoyed at close quarters.

ABOVE *Lilium regale AGM*

Popular species and varieties: The Asiatic hybrids are easy to grow, producing sturdy growth with stems some 36–48in (90–120cm) high, and upward-facing blooms. Flowering is from early to mid-summer. Look for: 'Sweet Kiss' (a deep reddish pink with a golden yellow centre); 'Orange Pixie' (a bright orange); 'Saidja' (dark red); 'Bach' (pure white); and 'Cote d'Azur' (deep pink, getting lighter towards the centre).

Some of the most dramatic of the hybrid lilies are in the group known as the Orientals. These boast some excellent fragrant varieties among their number, all flowering from mid-summer onwards. They are lime-haters, so if your soil is alkaline grow them in containers. Among the best are 'Arena', large white flowers with a yellow star in the centre, and 'Garden Party' AGM, white with a yellow stripe. 'Muscadet' has flowers of pure white, spotted with rose-red. Trumpet lilies have stout stems and large trumpet-shaped flowers. Most bloom in mid-summer. The rich orange flower buds of 'African Queen'

open to glossy glowing orange trumpets; 'Golden Splendour' is deep yellow, its huge flowers being held on 5ft (1.5m) stems. There are, it seems, just as many species of lily as there are hybrids. One of the best, and one of those most appreciating acid-soil conditions, is *L. longiflorum*, often called the Easter lily. It is one of the most perfect of white lilies, and has elongated petals. Beware however, for it hates windy conditions, and I have had most success with it in a pot – and in a conservatory!

Another acid-lover of note is the golden-rayed lily, *L. auratum*, a native of Japan; it has white, fragrant, saucer-shaped flowers, and each petal has a yellow band running along its length. Look out also for *L. auratum* var. *platyphyllum* AGM, with large waxy white flowers.

The Madonna lily (*L. candidum* AGM) produces strong 4ft (1.2m) high stems and carries fragrant pure white funnel-shaped flowers in early summer. These can be 6in (15cm) wide. This lily requires a warm sheltered position. It is basal rooting, and can be difficult to establish; once planted, do not disturb it.

The regal lily (*L. regale* AGM) is one of the best white funnel-shaped lilies. Its fragrant blooms in mid-summer can be 6in (15cm) long, with several on a stout stem. It does best in full sun, but tolerates dappled shade well.

NAME: NARCISSUS (DAFFODIL)

Origin: Southern Europe, Northern Africa, Western Asia, China, Japan
Type: Bulbous perennials
USDA Zone: Z4–9
Preferred pH range: 6.0–6.5
Description: The classic sign for most non-gardeners (and gardeners for that matter) that spring has arrived, is swathes of golden daffodils throwing out their glorious colour in parks, common land, roadside verges and, of course, gardens everywhere. All daffodils are forms – large-flowered hybrids, actually – of *Narcissus*. There are more than 50 species

of *Narcissus* and, literally, thousands of cultivars. These are among the most popular of hardy bulbs, and they range from miniature species and hybrids to tall cultivars with large flowers. Leaves are grass-like in the case of miniature species, otherwise they are strap-shaped. The flowers consist of a trumpet (or cup-shaped 'corona') surrounded by flat or reflexed petals (referred to by botanists as 'perianth segments'). Botanists have divided daffodils into 12 divisions   identified in brackets below, but it is not too important for gardeners to understand the distinctions. Incidentally, acid soils are favoured by nearly all narcissi – except for those varieties that come under Jonquilla (Division 7) and Tazetta (Division 8), which actually prefer a soil that is slightly alkaline.

Popular species and varieties: Listed below are one each from the ten divisions that comprise acid loving *Narcissus*. Look for: 'Mount Hood' (Division 1 – Daffodil) with broad, pure white petals and an ivory-white trumpet; 'Ice Follies' (2 – Large-cupped), a robust grower with pale yellow and white blooms; 'Merlin' AGM (3 – Small-cupped), pure white petals with a delicate bright yellow cup with a fine orange-red rim, green at the base; 'Tahiti' AGM (4 – Double) with golden-yellow and orange-red double flowers; 'Hawera' AGM (5 – Triandrus), two to six cream-yellow, slightly fragrant flowers per stem; 'Beryl' (6 – Cyclamineus), yellow and burnt orange on 8in (20cm) high stems; 'Actaea' (9 – Poeticus) with flowers of golden yellow and white, very fragrant; *Narcissus bulbocodium* (10 – Species and Wild Narcissus) is known as the hoop petticoat narcissus, with rich golden yellow funnel-shaped trumpets; 'Lemon Beauty' (11 – Split Corona), white with a yellow and white corona; and 'Tête-a-Tête' (12 – Others), a golden yellow, multi-headed dwarf *Narcissus* that is sold in flower by the million every springtime from garden centres.

ABOVE ***Narcissus bulbocodium***

BULBOUS PLANTS PREFERRING SOILS IN THE NEUTRAL RANGE

The following plants thrive in a soil with a pH range that straddles both the higher levels of acidity and the lower levels of alkalinity

Latin name	Common name	pH range
Amaryllis	Belladonna lily	5.5–7.5
Canna	Indian shot plant	6.0–7.5
Cardiocrinum	Giant lily	5.5–7.5
Dahlia	Dahlia	6.0–7.5
Erythronium	Dog's tooth violet	6.5–7.5
Freesia	Freesia	6.0–8.0
Fritillaria	Fritillary/Crown imperial	6.0–7.5
Hyacinthoides	Bluebell	6.0–7.5
Hyacinthus	Hyacinth	6.0–7.5
Leucojum	Snowflake	6.0–7.5
Muscari	Grape hyacinth	6.0–7.5
Nerine	Guernsey lily	6.5–7.5
Ornithogalum	Star of Bethlehem/Chincherinchee	6.5–7.5
Ranunculus	Buttercup	5.5–7.5
Rhodohypoxis	Rose grass	5.5–7.5
Schizostylis	Kaffir lily	5.5–7.5
Tecophilaea	Tecophilaea	6.5–7.5
Tigridia	Tiger flower	6.5–7.5
Tulipa	Tulip	6.0–7.5

ABOVE *Dahlia* 'Sonia'

ABOVE *Tulipa* 'Apricot Beauty' AGM

ABOVE *Canna* 'Picasso' AGM

ABOVE *Erythronium* 'Kondo'

ABOVE *Cardiocrinum giganteum*

PERENNIALS

NAME: *ACANTHUS* (BEAR'S BREECHES)

Origin: Mediterranean region, tropical Africa and Australia
Type: Hardy perennial
USDA Zone: Z7
Preferred pH range: 6.0–7.0
Description: These plants need space in which to be appreciated; they are vigorous enough to steadily expand and smother nearby neighbours. Although the leaves appear to be spiny, they are in fact soft and harmless. The flowers, however, are a different matter, the individual blooms each being protected by a sharp spine. Plants produce flower spikes some 4–5ft (1.2–1.5m) tall, and an established clump will continue to flower more or less from early summer to late autumn.

Popular species and varieties: *Acanthus spinosus* AGM is the best-known form, and is hardly distinguishable from *A. mollis*, its close cousin. The latter is slightly less free to flower and needs a warmer spot in which to thrive. *A. hungaricus* has handsome foliage and produces 3–4ft (1–1.2m) tall spikes of lilac-mauve flowers. The smallest is the slow-growing *A. dioscoridis* var. *perringii*, which has greyish leaves and occasional spikes 12in (30cm) high, carrying pinkish flowers.

NAME: *ACONITUM* (MONKSHOOD)

Origin: Throughout the northern hemisphere
Type: Hardy perennials
USDA Zone: Z3–6
Preferred pH range: 5.0–6.0
Description: The hooded flowers of the aconites are very distinctive, and have caused plants to be given several common names, including monkshood, helmet flower and wolf's bane. Flowers are most commonly blue or violet, and sometimes white, pink and soft yellow. While they are at their best in an open, sunny position, provided a plentiful supply of moisture is present, they will also grow well in a lightly shaded spot. All parts of the *Aconitum* plant are poisonous, but especially the roots. It is thought that these plants were first brought into gardens for this very reason, perhaps for use as poison for arrow heads.

Popular species and varieties: There are several excellent garden hybrids: *Aconitum* x *cammarum* 'Bicolor' AGM, as its name

ABOVE *Acanthus spinosus* AGM

108

suggests, has a distinctive combination of blue and white on branching stems. 'Spark's Variety' AGM was first introduced in the nineteenth century and has stood the test of time with its dark violet-blue flowers. 'Ivorine' is a vigorous, bushy plant with ivory white flowers on branching stems. *A. japonicum* produces deep violet-blue flowers, which really stand out against the vivid greenery of the leaves. *A. carmichaelii* has tuberous roots and produces a mass of blue flowers; the best form is undoubtedly 'Arendsii' AGM, with lavender-blue flowers.

NAME: *ACORUS*
(SWEET FLAG, OR SWEET RUSH)

Origin: North America, Asia, Europe
Type: Hardy moisture-loving perennial
USDA Zone: 74–5
Preferred pH range: 5.0–6.5
Description: This is a grass-like moisture-lover with aromatic foliage but insignificant flowers. Technically this is neither a grass, nor a bamboo, yet it has the appearance of both. It is actually a member of the *Arum* family, its flower being a spathe and typical of this particular plant family. The narrow, flat, grass-like leaves come from the root area in a distinct fan-shape, unlike any grass. Members of the genus are to be found close to water.

Popular species and varieties: *Acorus gramineus* 'Variegatus' has green leaves with a central white stripe; 'Oborozuki' has yellow-gold leaves with slight green striping, and 'Ogon' is half-green, half-white. The green leaves of *A. calamus* will reach 18in (45cm) in length. The form 'Argentiostriatus' (often sold as 'Variegatus') has leaves of half-green and half cream. The cream part may be tinged pink if the plant is being stressed, such as when it is too dry or too cool.

RIGHT *Acorus gramineus* **'Variegatus'**

ABOVE *Aconitum japonicum*

ABOVE *Agapanthus campanulatus* 'Profusion'

NAME: *AGAPANTHUS* (AFRICAN LILY)

Origin: South Africa
Type: Hardy and tender perennials
USDA Zone: Z7–9
Preferred pH range: 5.5–6.5
Description: These are splendid plants for mid- to late summer colour; they are successful in borders and also ideal subjects for a large container alongside a path or on the patio. Native to South Africa, in time they form compact clumps. The roots are fleshy and require protection in cold districts. Choose a sheltered spot in full sun. Alternatively, grow them in a large tub that can be moved as required. The *Agapanthus* is ideal for growing in pots for keeping in a cold greenhouse or conservatory. These plants have strap-shaped mid-green foliage. Some are deciduous, others evergreen.
Popular species and varieties: Among the best-known members of this family are the 'Headbourne Hybrids'. Colours vary from deep violet to pale blue, and the flowers are held on stout stems of 24–30in (60–75cm) high. These hybrids are generally hardier than the species. One form that never fails to attract attention when in full bloom is the pale blue *A. campanulatus* subsp. *patens* AGM. As with all members of this family it hates root disturbance; once planted it is best left alone. It will, in time, build into a sizeable clump, with mauve flowers. Another good choice is *A. campanulatus* 'Profusion' with large rounded dark blue flowerheads in mid-summer. While varieties have flowers of varying shades of blue, those with pure white blooms should not be forgotten. Among the best is 'White Superior'; with dense flower clusters carried on strong, 28in (70cm) high stems.

NAME: *AJUGA* (BUGLE)

Origin: Europe, Middle East
Type: Hardy perennial
USDA Zone: Z6
Preferred pH range: 4.0–6.0
Description: These are hardy, often vigorous plants that flower in spring or early summer, in an increasing range of forms with coloured and variegated foliage. Ajugas make excellent ground-cover plants, with their short spikes of blue or pink flowers covering quite an area in time. They like a moist, relatively strongly acidic soil, and will tolerate dappled shade (the deeper the shade the less flowers will be produced, and the more likely that coloured leaved forms will revert to all-green).
Popular species and varieties: *Ajuga reptans* produces flowers of Royal blue over deep green leaves. Varieties bred for their rich leaf colourings, including 'Arctic Fox' (cream leaves with dark green edges), 'Braunherz' AGM (deep purple bronze) and 'Burgundy Glow' AGM (maroon and cream, and light blue flowers); both grow to just 6in (15cm) or so in height. 'Catlin's Giant' AGM reaches 10in (25cm). 'Vanilla Chip' has small green leaves with cream-white margins.

ABOVE *Ajuga reptans* 'Braunherz' AGM

NAME: *ALCHEMILLA MOLLIS* AGM (LADY'S MANTLE)

Origin: Worldwide, but most garden forms are of European origin
Type: Hardy perennial
USDA Zone: Z5–7
Preferred pH range: 6.0–7.0
Description: This plant has handsome green foliage and masses of yellow-green, feathery sprays of flowers that are carried over several weeks from early summer onwards. *Alchemilla* is a plant beloved of garden designers as the colour of leaves and flowers is such that it simply does not 'clash' in terms of colour, with any other plant. It is ideal for cutting and widely used by flower arrangers. The plant self-seeds, and once you have it you will find it cropping up in various places in the garden, some of them a surprising distance from the mother plant.
Popular species and varieties: *Alchemilla mollis* AGM is the form most commonly found. 'Auslese' is more pleated, grey-green colour and needs light shade in order to perform in its optimum way. 'Robusta' is slightly taller, possibly up to 30in (75cm), and 'Variegata' has leaves that are randomly accented with yellow markings.

ABOVE *Alchemilla mollis* AGM

111

ABOVE *Aquilegia 'Georgia' State Series*

NAME: *AQUILEGIA* (COLUMBINE)

Origin: Throughout the northern hemisphere
Type: Hardy perennial
USDA Zone: Z3–4
Preferred pH range: 6.0–7.0
Description: Aquilegias are elegant, bright and cheerful flowers that bring glamour and charm to the early summer garden. Although there are around 70 species to choose from, only a handful are commonly seen in gardens. They also seed themselves generously around the garden, and I don't know any gardeners who have them and who resent this trait. Aquilegias grow up to 3ft (90cm) or so. After two or three years the flower production starts to decline, and it is worth buying or sowing new replacement plants.

Popular species and varieties: The McKana Strain of very long-spurred aquilegias are graceful additions to almost any garden site, and will even tolerate some shade. The Winky series is a bit of fun, with picotee flowers that appear from a distance as though they are members of the *Dianthus* (pinks) family; look for the forms sold by colour, such as 'Red-White', 'Purple-White' and 'Pink'. 'Hensol Harebell' AGM is a name that strictly belongs to a strain of blues. An excellent series is the State series, named after US states. Amongst others, look for 'Alaska' (all white), 'Colorado' (violet and white), 'Florida' (all yellow) and 'Georgia' (red and white).

NAME: *ASPLENIUM* (SPLEENWORT)

Origin: Worldwide, from temperate and tropical regions
Type: Hardy fern
USDA Zone: Z3–5
Preferred pH range: 5.0–5.5
Description: These are compact, occasionally creeping plants carrying usually evergreen fronds, which vary considerably in shape. The fronds are generally slightly leathery in texture. Aspleniums are defined by their elongated spore-bearing areas, which, in most species, are formed individually along the frond segments. The species have a tendency to hybridize with each other, and other fern genera, resulting in some interesting mixed hybrids.

Popular species and varieties: *Asplenium scolopendrium* AGM is the hart's tongue fern. It is a very distinctive plant with undivided fronds. Especially lovely when new, the fronds do maintain a very dressy appearance for months and, in a sheltered spot, can be one of the most attractive ferns for the winter period. Crispum Group is a small range of very similar ferns but these are sterile. The frond margins are beautifully crimped into a ruff.

ABOVE *Asplenium scolopendrium* Crispum Group

NAME: *ASTILBE*

Origin: Eastern Asia, North America
Type: Hardy perennial
USDA Zone: Z5–6
Preferred pH range: 5.5–7.0
Description: These are graceful, colourful and hardy mid-summer flowers for bold planting in moist situations. Without moisture – and a little shade – they can fall well short of their display potential. The attractive plume-like heads of tiny flowers, which last for several weeks, ensure that the *Astilbe* owner has a good return on their investment. The rusty-brown seedheads produced in late summer and autumn are almost as effective as the flower spikes. Although tough little plants, they may suffer superficial damage to young shoots if there is a heavy spring frost.
Popular species and varieties: *Astilbe* x *arendsii* has produced many beautiful hybrids, generally producing plumes up to 3ft (1m) in height. 'Bressingham Beauty' is bright pink, 'Anita Pfeifer' is sugar-pink, 'Harmony' is candyfloss pink and 'Amethyst' is lilac-purple. 'Fire' is often found under its German name 'Feuer', and produces a

ABOVE *Astilbe* x *arendsii* 'Feuer'

brilliant red flower. The species *A. simplicifolia* has added its quota too. 'Atrorosea' carries sheaves of tiny bright pink flowers over a long period. 'Bronce Elegans' AGM is a charming dark-leafed pink variety only 9in (23cm) high. 'Hennie Graafland' has dark glossy green leaves and light, purplish-pink flowers.

ABOVE *Campanula* 'Kent Belle' AGM

NAME: *CAMPANULA* (BELLFLOWER)

Origin: Worldwide
Type: Hardy perennial
USDA Zone: Z3–5
Preferred pH range: 5.5–6.5
Description: This is a large and diverse group of showy, spring- and summer-flowering plants for a sunny or shady border. Over 300 species exist, including the biennial Canterbury bells (*Campanula media*). The colours are predominantly blues and mauves, but there are excellent pinks and whites too. Some of the smaller campanulas are suitable for growing in containers and recent introductions have been made with this in mind.
Popular species and varieties: The so-called clustered bellflower, *Campanula glomerata* 'Superba' AGM, has deep violet flowers on 3ft (90cm) high stems in summer. The form 'Joan Elliott' is the same colour, but on shorter stems and flowers a few weeks earlier. *C. alliariifolia* has white flowers, although there are forms with cream shades. *C. lactiflora* is a most valuable, tall perennial – at 5ft (1.5m) or so – so will need staking. It has lavender-blue flowers on leafy stems. Look also for 'Loddon Anna' AGM (pink), 'Pritchard's Variety' AGM (pale purple) and 'Alba' (pure white). 'Kent Belle' AGM carries a mass of heart-shaped leaves, and loose clusters of nodding, shiny, violet-blue bells.

NAME: *CENTAUREA* (KNAPWEED OR CORNFLOWER)

Origin: The Mediterranean region and Western Asia
Type: Hardy perennial
USDA Zone: Z3–6
Preferred pH range: 5.0–7.0
Description: These are perfect plants if you have a poor, hot, dry soil, and you want to encourage plenty of bees and butterflies to your garden. Although generally regarded as acid-loving plants, they can occasionally, for no explicable reason, be surprisingly tolerant of lime. The excellent *Centaurea ruthenica* is one species that actually prefers a limy soil.
Popular species and varieties: *Centaurea montana* is known variously as the perennial

ABOVE *Centaurea montana* 'Carnea'

ABOVE **Marguerites are still known by many as chrysanthemums, but now are more correctly referred to as *Argyranthemum frutescens*.**

cornflower, or mountain bluet. Several very good cultivars have come from it. 'Alba' is white, but often with a pinkish tinge, 'Carnea' is mauve-pink, 'Parham' is lavender-blue and 'Violetta' has flowers of deep violet-red. *C. cineraria* subsp. *cineraria* AGM produces lovely intricately cut silvery (or downy) foliage. It is used extensively in bedding schemes, for its bright leaf colour stands out well against strong bedding flowers next to it. When used in such a way it is grown as an annual, with fresh seed sown in spring; however, this is a perennial and can give a good account of itself over several years. Discard it after four years.

NAME: *CHRYSANTHEMUM*

Origin: Central and Eastern Asia, Europe
Type: Hardy and tender perennials
USDA Zone: Z5–7
Preferred pH range: 6.0–7.0
Description: Where does one start to talk about chrysanthemums? First off, there is confusion over the names; our fathers and grandfathers would have been able to spot a *Chrysanthemum* a mile off but today, after botanists and plant registrars have done their deeds, these plants may be listed under any of the following genera: *Dendranthema* (mainly), as well as *Ajania*, *Leucanthemum*, *Leucanthemella*, *Nipponanthemum*, *Rhodanthemum* and *Tanacetum*. There was uproar when the names were changed, mainly from the commercial garden *Chrysanthemum* sector, which maintained that the name *Dendranthema* would go unrecognized by gardeners and consumers.

ABOVE *Chrysanthemum rubellum* 'Emperor of China'

ABOVE *Chrysanthemum* 'Manderin'

They claimed that this would lead to a huge loss of income and revenue for horticulture in general. So the original name for most of the popular garden forms has reverted to *Chrysanthemum*; the various other new genus names still apply to certain types (mainly the less popular or rare forms), and the continued use of the new names for these has largely gone unnoticed.

To add to the confusion, there are so many different forms and styles of the garden chrysanthemums that the National Chrysanthemum Society in England, recognized as the world authority, has created a system of classification codes as a simple differentiator. Gardeners growing just a few perennial plants rarely need to know or use these codes, for most apply just to the varieties grown for showing at exhibition. Garden chrysanthemums – half-hardy to hardy perennials – really epitomize autumn with their wide range of colours. The flowers of all types are excellent for cutting. In terms of cultivation, you should pinch out the tips of young plants to encourage branching; side shoots can also be pinched out.

Provide supports for tall chrysanthemums. In mid- or late autumn cut stems down to 6in (15cm), and store the crowns of the plants in trays of potting compost in a frost-free greenhouse over winter.

Popular species and varieties: The most commonly seen forms are: hardy Rubellum hybrids (especially good for mixed borders, and plants can be left in the ground all year round); the earlier-flowering florists' chrysanthemums, such as the Sprays (grown in borders, too, but generally not so hardy); and the hardy dwarf kinds, especially the Pompons (ideal for patio tubs as well as mixed borders).

The lovely old cottage-garden plants known as Marguerites, whereas previously chrysanthemums, now sit within the genus *Argyranthemum* (although few gardeners have yet learned to call them by their new name). As for the garden hybrid and 'pot' mums, there are far too many cultivars and it does not seem appropriate to list even one or two here. They also go in and out of fashion, so you would be far better to consult a specialist's catalogue.

NAME: *CORYDALIS*

Origin: Europe, Asia, Tropical Africa
Type: Hardy perennial
USDA Zone: Z5–7
Preferred pH range: 6.0–7.0
Description: Dwarf, hardy spring-flowering perennials, with attractive, long-lasting tubular flowers. The first forms to be grown were yellow, but plant breeders discovered there was a good market for these plants, and that it was relatively easy to breed new colours into them. Suitable for rock and alpine gardens, lightly shaded borders and, perhaps most appropriately of all, the partial shade of woodland gardens. Slugs and snails are the main problems.
Popular species and varieties: *Corydalis solida* is a clump-forming plant growing from small underground tubers. In mid-spring spikes of pink, mauve, white or reddish-purple flowers appear, accompanied by attractive grey-green leaves. An excellent form of this is *C. solida* subsp. *incisa*

AGM, with flowers of white or very pale purple, and *C. solida* subsp. *solida* 'George Baker' AGM, with flowers of an unusual brick-red colour. *C. solida* subsp. *solida* 'Dieter Schacht' AGM is compact and has flowers of light pink flushed deeper pink on the lips, whilst *C. solida* subsp. *solida* 'Beth Evans' is white to very pale pink. *C. flexuosa* has dark, finely cut foliage and blue-spurred flowers. There are several varieties available, including: 'China Blue' (light blue flowers); 'Purple Leaf' (blue-mauve flowers with a purplish tinge to the leaves); and 'Golden Panda' (blue flowers with yellow leaves at their brightest in spring). *C. lutea*, with yellow flowers, is one of those plants that once you have in the garden you are unlikely to lose, for it seeds itself prodigiously. It is also evergreen, providing useful cover in winter. One hybrid worth mentioning is *C.* 'Blackberry Wine', a vigorous plant forming a clump of blue-green leaves topped from mid spring to late summer with purplish-pink flowers.

ABOVE *Corydalis solida*

ABOVE *Gentiana* 'Marsha'

NAME: *GENTIANA* (GENTIAN)

Origin: North America, Europe, Eastern Asia, Himalayas, New Zealand
Type: Hardy perennial
USDA Zone: Z3–6
Preferred pH range: 5.0–7.0
Description: Elegant summer- or autumn-flowering plants valued for their often vivid blue flowers, gentians are some of the most admired plants for a rock garden. The characteristic trumpet-shaped gentian flower is legendary; although blue mainly, it is also possible to grow white, yellow, purple and red forms as well. Gentians have a reputation for being difficult to grow and even more difficult to flower but this is not true of all species. Most are best shaded from the strongest sun, unless summers are cool and moist. Provide humus-rich, steadily moist, acidic soils between pH5.0–7.0, and ensure good drainage for the small autumn-flowering mountain gentians.
Popular species and varieties: *Gentiana makinoi* produces blue flowers at the tips of 24in (60cm) long stems in summer. A new cultivar that has been winning awards is 'Marsha', with the brightest blue of any gentian. *G. sino-ornata* AGM produces its single blue flowers on creeping stems in autumn. The willow gentian (*G. asclepiadea* AGM) has blue flowers in its leaf axils on arching stems, whilst *G. septemfida* keeps low, with tufts of blue trumpet flowers throughout summer and autumn. The cultivar 'Alba' has white flowers, whilst *G. septemfida* var. *lagodechiana* AGM produces ground-hugging stems, each bearing one to three blue flowers.

NAME: *LUPINUS* (LUPIN)

Origin: The American continent, the Mediterranean region, North Africa
Type: Hardy perennial
USDA Zone: Z3–4
Preferred pH range: 5.5–7.0
Description: Iconic cottage garden plants, lupins are derived from the species *Lupinus polyphyllus*, with flower spikes reaching some 3–4ft (90–120cm). There are around 200 species in total, but these comprise annuals, biennials and shrubs in addition to perennials. The 'Russell' lupins are the best known, first developed in the 1930s, and now the named forms of these are far more widely grown than the species. The generally dense flower spikes come in a spectacular range of shades, including varying tones of blue, red, yellow, orange, pink, lilac and white. There are also plenty of bi-coloured varieties where the standard (inner petals) are a different colour or shade to the wings (outer petals). Lupins are always at their best in early summer. However, they are only short-lived, and need replacing every few years.

ABOVE *Lupinus* 'Gallery Blue Shades'

Many find lupins fail on them, probably because they are prone to a number of ailments: slugs, snails, powdery mildew, aphids, anthracnose disease and various virus diseases may attack. If you manage to avoid these problems your plants can give you tremendous pleasure.

Popular species and varieties: . For blue, look for 'Blue Jacket' and 'Freedom'; for violet try 'Saxby'. For yellow, look for 'Canary Bird'; in 'Brightness' and 'Catherine of York' it is mixed with pink. For orange, look for 'Lulu'; and for pink look for 'Helen Sharman'. The Band of Nobles Series AGM produces flowers in a range of colours, including 'Chandelier' (yellow), 'My Castle' (brick and dark red), 'The Governor' (blue and white with purple markings) and 'The Page' (carmine-red). Modern seed strains – such as 'Gallery Blue Shades' – are strong, sturdy plants producing broader, shorter flower spikes that breed true to colour.

ABOVE *Molinia caerulea* 'Variegata' AGM

NAME: *MOLINIA* (MOOR GRASS)

Origin: Throughout Europe to western Russia, and east to Japan

Type: Perennial grass

USDA Zone: Z4

Preferred pH range: 4.0–5.0

Description: These are elegant and valuable late-flowering ornamental grasses with tall, arching sprays of flowers. Clump-forming plants, they have a dense root system and green, pointed deciduous leaves; the flower stems are swollen at the base and appear in late summer. It is a handsome grass and looks particularly good moving in the breeze, especially in a mixed border. In autumn the leaves turn to bright oranges and russets.

Popular species and varieties: *Molinia caerulea* (purple moor grass, or purple melick) used to be divided into sub-species, but in recent years botanists at the Royal Botanic Gardens at Kew in England have come to the conclusion that the two sub-species are one and the same. The confusion arose because in its natural habitats the grass appeared to look different when grown in the middle of an acid peat bog, to when it was growing on the drier fringes. This straight species has leaves of bright mid-green, opening from bright yellow shoots. 'Carmarthen' has pale green leaves striped cream-yellow; 'Edith Dudzus' has green leaves on reddish-purple stems; and 'Variegata' AGM has erect yellow and cream striped leaves.

NAME: *PENSTEMON* (BEARD TONGUE)

Origin: North and Central America

Type: Hardy perennial

USDA Zone: Z6–8

Preferred pH range: 5.5–7.0

Description: Arched sprays of cylindrical flowers adding drama and colour to summer beds and borders, herbaceous penstemons comprise some 250 species, of which only a handful have been used to breed the commonly seen garden forms. These plants are hardy everywhere, but they may be cut annually to the ground by frosts in cold districts (elsewhere they are evergreen). As a general rule the larger the leaves and flowers, the less hardy the variety.

Popular species and varieties: Look for 'Schoenholzeri' AGM (intense cerise), 'Apple Blossom' AGM (pink) and 'Sour Grapes' AGM (a sort of puce). 'Garnet' AGM (which may be found under its newer, but far less memorable name 'Andenken an Friedrich Hahn') has deep burgundy flowers of good size, and is a bushy, compact grower that does not sprawl, as some cultivars of *Penstemon* do. Gardeners should also be aware of the many hundreds of other penstemons that are available, in particular the many small alpine types such as *P. campanulatus*, a semi-evergreen with lavender and white flowers on wiry stems, and

P. heterophyllus (the so-called foothill penstemon) with bluish-green leaves and rose-violet funnel-shaped flowers that are produced in profusion.

NAME: *PERSICARIA BISTORTA* (BISTORT OR KNOTWEED)

Origin: China and the Himalayas
Type: Hardy perennial
USDA Zone: Z4–8
Preferred pH range: 5.5–7.0
Description: These are sturdy but attractive, long-flowering moisture-loving plants. They include some fine border perennials for carefree, late summer colour, and they also include in their number a few reasonably pernicious weeds. In fact, one of the worst and most vigorous of plants that has become a weed of such magnitude that whole companies have been formed with the purpose of eradicating it – Japanese knotweed used to be in the *Persicaria* genus, but it has now been given its own name of *Fallopia*. Many of the plants older gardeners will know as *Polygonum* are also now in the *Persicaria* genus.

Popular species and varieties: The common bistort (*Persicaria bistorta*) produces wavy-edged leaves and non-branching stems containing at their tips pale pink flowers clustered into dense, fluffy bottlebrushes. The red bistort (*P. amplexicaulis*) is a vigorous plant producing considerable quantities of small, heart-shaped leaves, which makes it good for ground cover. The usually reddish flower spikes start in early summer and come in succession until mid-autumn. Look for 'Atrosanguinea' (deep purple-red flowers); 'Cottesbrooke Gold' (pinkish red flowers over yellow to lime foliage); 'Firetail' AGM (long, tapering spikes of bright red); and 'Alba' (white).

TOP RIGHT *Penstemon* 'Andenken an Friedrich Hahn' AGM (syn. 'Garnet')

RIGHT *Persicaria bistorta*

ABOVE *Phlox* 'Chattahoochee' AGM

NAME: *PHLOX*

Origin: North America
Type: Hardy perennial
USDA Zone: Z3–6
Preferred pH range: 6.0–7.0
Description: Phlox fill the summer air with perfume, and delight the eye with a kaleidoscope of colours. Plants in this genus are free-flowering and are perfect for 'cottage gardens' adjoining older properties. They are subject to bad attacks of mildew in certain years, but some varieties are more robust than others, and the varieties listed below are the most trouble-free I've grown or come across. There are over 60 species (comprising both annuals and perennials) and with careful selection of varieties you can have them in flower from early summer through to mid-autumn.

Popular species and varieties: Most border forms are from *Phlox paniculata*. 'Amethyst' has flowers of a deep lilac. 'Prospero' AGM is lilac tinged with white. 'Flamingo' has pink flowers with magenta 'eyes'. But arguably the best of all is 'Mount Fuji' AGM; it is late flowering, right into mid-autumn, and its outstanding free-flowering and robust nature combine with the purity of its white flowers to make an unbeatable perennial. There are several variegated phloxes, including 'Norah Leigh' and 'Harlequin'.

Smaller plants, best suited to the rock garden, include forms of the so-called blue phlox (*P. divaricata*). Look for 'Chattahoochee' AGM (also known as 'Moody Blue'), with lavender-blue flowers with cerise eyes; and 'White Perfume', fragrant white flowers with narrow petals.

NAME: *POLYSTICHUM* (SHIELD FERN)

Origin: Most of the temperate regions of the world

Type: Hardy fern

USDA Zone: Z3–8

Preferred pH range: 4.5–6.0

Description: Among the most handsome of hardy ferns, these plants give all-season interest in the garden. There are probably as many as 300 species found in the wild across the world, but only ten or so, with cultivars, are commonly found in gardens. In most garden-worthy types the young growth in spring is conspicuous and attractive with its covering of gingery or silvery scales. The spore-bearing organs on the underside of the frond are covered by a round, shield-shaped structure attached in the centre, hence the common name.

Popular species and varieties: Some 15 species and 30 cultivars are available, but they all appear much the same – unless you are a pteridologist (an expert in the study of ferns). *P. aculeatum* forms a round clump of fronds, usually 2–3ft (60–90cm) across, and in maturity is a rich, dark green. The soft shield fern (*P. setiferum*) is bigger at some 5ft (1.5m) long; *P. setiferum* 'Acutilobum' has narrow, more pointed fronds. Finally, apple-green fronds that are upright, and more densely leafy towards the base, are to be found in *P. setiferum* Dahlem Group.

ABOVE *Polystichum setiferum* 'Acutilobum'

ABOVE *Primula denticulata var. alba*

NAME: *PRIMULA* (PRIMROSE)

Origin: Throughout the northern hemisphere, southern South America

Type: Hardy perennials

USDA Zone: Z5–6

Preferred pH range: 5.5–6.5

Description: This genus comprises more than 450 species, but only 30 of these are important today as garden plants. However, from this 30 have derived hundreds of different named cultivars, and there is something in them to please every gardener. Primulas are mainly hardy herbaceous and evergreen perennials. There are types for growing in pots, on rockeries, in flowerbeds, in woodland dells and at the sides of a pond. They prefer a fairly rich, organic soil. Whichever plants you grow in your acid-soil garden there should be room for a patch of primulas. Slightly shaded places are even better for them. Only those generally considered perennials, rather than alpines requiring frost protection, are considered here.

Popular species and varieties: *Primula japonica* is possibly the best known of the 'candelabra' primulas (meaning that it bears its flowers in rounded clusters, or whorls, at intervals along the main central stem). It produces lush mid-green leaves and several tiers of flowers in white, red or pink; these open at stages throughout early and mid-summer. Four of the best varieties are: 'Apple Blossom' (pink); 'Carminea' (dark reddish flowers with a darker eye and paler foliage); 'Miller's Crimson' (deep pink); and 'Postford White' (white). Other candelabra primulas include *P. aurantiaca* (orange, or orange-red), *P. beesiana* (deep red with yellow centres), *P. x bulleesiana* (in a wide range of colours from yellow, orange and pink through to red and purple) and *P. pulverulenta* (pale pink or mauve). The drumstick primula (*P. denticulata*) has deciduous, rough, leathery leaves; its flowers open in late winter or early spring and are usually lilac-blue, and are carried in a tight, globular head. *P. denticulata* var. *alba* is pure white (sometimes going under the cultivar name 'Snowball'). 'Glenroy Crimson' is another excellent form of the drumstick primula, this time with flowers of deep red. The relatively small flowers of the Gold Laced Group are dark red to deep chocolate brown, with each petal edged in golden yellow; it's a stunning plant for a cool, damp sot in part shade. The common or wild primrose (*P. vulgaris*) makes a fine addition to any garden, but is perhaps most at home in a wild area in longish, uncut grass and dappled shade. The blooms of *P. vulgaris* subsp. *sibthorpii* are pink, or occasionally white. There are so many other forms to consider, it is worth finding a specialist supplier and consulting their catalogue.

NAME: *PULSATILLA* (PASQUE FLOWER)

Origin: Mountain slopes throughout Europe, North America and Asia
Type: Hardy perennial
USDA Zone: 25
Preferred pH range: 5.0–6.0
Description: These cute members of the buttercup family produce showy flowers, ferny foliage and silvery seedheads – combining to make a delightful combination for a border in full sun. Compact clumps of often very hairy deciduous leaves arise each spring, and a month or so later large, handsome bell-shaped and sometimes star-shaped flowers appear. Each flower has a bold yellow centre. By mid-summer these flowers have usually given way to attractive, feathery seedheads.
Popular species and varieties: *Pulsatilla vulgaris* AGM is the only species that is widely available, but it has given rise to a number of excellent cultivars. The straight species has bell-shaped flowers of pink-purple, but the following cultivars are certainly worth garden space: 'Alba' AGM (white); 'Barton's Pink' (clear pink); 'Blau Glocke' (lilac-blue); and 'Eva Constance' (deep red).

ABOVE *Pulsatilla vulgaris* **AGM**

ABOVE *Trillium chloropetalum*

NAME: *TRILLIUM* (WOOD LILY)

Origin: North-eastern Asia, Himalayas, North America

Type: Rhizomatous perennials

USDA Zone: Z4–6

Preferred pH range: 5.0–6.5

Description: This is one of the few herbaceous perennials that almost should be classed as a bulbous plant; in fact many authorities insist that it is (*Agapanthus* and *Eranthis* provoke similar debates). The roots are somewhat bulb-like, semi-upright underground stems, or rhizomes. The common name 'wood lily' does the *Trillium* a disservice. These are fabulous plants that can carpet a dappled glade with colour in spring. My personal favourites are the whites, but there are also purples, creams and greenish-yellows. As the genus name suggests, the blooms are made up of three petals. They are all bent backwards slightly, and are carried on stems 12in (30cm) or so high. Different species tend to have different common names, often with such endearing names as the whippoorwill flower (*Trillium cuneatum*), white toadshade (*T. albidum*) and wake robin (*T. grandiflorum*).

Popular species and varieties: *Trillium sessile* has leaves of deep green, marbled grey. The usually maroon flowers are stemless, narrow, erect and pointed with slightly twisted petals. The stems are slightly shorter, at 10–12in (20–30cm), and are produced from late spring. *T. chloropetalum* has mottled leaves and cream-white flowers, whilst *T. luteum* has greenish-yellow blooms. *T. erectum* is a curious member of the family; with the common name of birthroot, or squawroot, it produces bright maroon-purple spring flowers and large three-lobed mid-green leaves. Some of the best colour and drama comes from *Trillium grandiflorum* AGM, the most widely grown species. It is best in shady spots beneath deciduous trees. Flowers are pure white, and even better is the double form 'Flore Pleno' AGM (a very desirable plant, and for this reason is more expensive to buy). Also look for *T. grandiflorum* f. *roseum*, with flowers of varying shades of pink.

126

PERENNIALS PREFERRING SOILS IN THE NEUTRAL RANGE

The following plants thrive in a soil with a pH range that straddles both the higher levels of acidity and the lower levels of alkalinity

Latin name	Common name	pH range
Androsace	Rock jasmine	5.0–7.5
Bletilla	Hardy orchid	6.0–7.5
Cautleya	–	5.5–7.5
Cerastium	Snow-in-summer	6.0–7.5
Corynephorus	Hair grass	5.5–7.5
Dactylorhiza	Marsh orchid	5.5–7.5
Epimedium	Barrenwort	6.0–7.5
Eranthis	Winter aconite	6.0–8.0
Euphorbia	Spurge	6.0–7.5
Glaucidium	–	6.0–7.5
Gymnocarpium	Oak fern	5.5–7.5
Jeffersonia	Twin leaf	5.5–7.5
Mimulus	Monkey flower/Musk flower	6.0–7.5
Parahebe	–	6.0–7.5
Phlegopteris	Beech fern	5.5–7.5
Roscoea	–	5.5–7.5
Schoenoplectus	Bullrush/Club rush	5.5–7.5
Semiaquilegia	–	6.0–7.5
Solidago	Golden rod	5.5–7.5
Veronica	Speedwell	5.5–7.5

ABOVE **Bletilla striata 'Albostriata'**

ABOVE **Epimedium sagittatum**

ABOVE **Eranthis hyemalis AGM**

TREES, SHRUBS AND CLIMBERS

ABOVE *Acer palmatum* var. *dissectum* Dissectum Atropurpureum Group

NAME: *ACER* (JAPANESE MAPLE)

Origin: North and Central America, Europe, North Africa, Asia

Type: Deciduous or evergreen trees and shrubs

USDA Zone: Z2–8

Preferred pH range: 5.5–7.0

Description: Some acers can develop into large trees, but any of the garden-worthy Japanese maples are low shrubs. The smaller forms are valuable for giving scale to plantings on a rockery, or for tumbling over a low wall. Most make good structural plantings in the garden, whether for foliage (especially autumn colour) or their barks. When leaves are young they can be scorched if the sun is too strong, so it is often a good idea to grow them in containers, so that you can move them from a semi-shaded spot into a sunny one when the leaves have fully developed and thickened.

Popular species and varieties: 'Bloodgood' AGM is a superb taller species. It has lobed dark red-purple foliage that turns to bright red in autumn. Mature specimens can reach 16ft (5m) or more in height. Slightly taller at 20ft (6m) is 'Osakazuki' AGM, which produces fiery red foliage in autumn. Among the Dissectum Group of *Acer palmatum* – all with a shrubby habit and finely divided foliage – is 'Viride' with bright green leaves, and 'Atropurpureum' (bronze-red). 'Garnet' AGM is a good choice with reddish-purple foliage. 'Red Pygmy' has reddish-purple leaves with long, slender lobes. There are many other excellent forms within this Group, and all are suited to the smaller garden.

128

NAME: *ANDROMEDA* (BOG ROSEMARY)

Origin: Arctic, Temperate northern hemisphere
Type: Evergreen shrubs
USDA Zone: Z2
Preferred pH range: 5.5–7.0
Description: This plant is a natural choice for the acid garden. A dwarf evergreen shrub, it is a rare native to Britain, and has rosemary-like foliage and clusters of bell-shaped, pink flowers in late spring.
Popular species and varieties: *Andromeda polifolia* 'Alba' and *A. polifolia* 'Compacta' AGM bearing, respectively, white and pink flowers on compact plants, are the best choices for most gardens.

NAME: *ARAUCARIA ARAUCANA* (MONKEY PUZZLE OR CHILE PINE)

Origin: Chile
Type: Evergreen conifer
USDA Zone: Z8–10
Preferred pH range: 5.0–6.0
Description: This curious tree makes a fine specimen in a lawn, but looks incongruous when grown in a border and surrounded by other plants. Initially slow growing, it has an open habit when young, the trunk and branches densely clothed in radially arranged sharp, spiny, dark green leaves that point forward along the stems. This gives the tree its common name (in that a monkey, it is thought, would be unable to climb up it). Plants can live for hundreds of years.
Popular species and varieties: *Araucaria araucana* is the most frequently seen species by far. The Norfolk Island pine (*A. heterophylla*) is a beautiful tree which, in a cool climate, can be grown as a house or conservatory plant – until it gets too big.

TOP RIGHT *Andromeda polifolia* 'Compacta' AGM
RIGHT *Araucaria araucana*

129

ABOVE *Arbutus unedo*

NAME: *ARBUTUS UNEDO* (KILLARNEY STRAWBERRY TREE)

Origin: North and Central America, south and western Europe, Middle East

Type: Evergreen trees

USDA Zone: Z6–8

Preferred pH range: 4.0–7.0

Description: This is an ornamental, slim, spreading tree with dark green, glossy leaves. When fully grown it often becomes gnarled, with a beautiful stem of deep reddish-brown, shredding bark. Small white, hanging cup-shaped flowers are carried at the same time as the strawberry-like fruits, in late autumn. Although a member of the heather and rhododendron family, preferring an acid soil, it has been known in some cases to tolerate slightly alkaline soils – but not exclusively so you should be aware that it may not survive in a soil with a pH higher than 7.0. In Latin 'unedo' means 'eat one', for if you eat just one of the berries the taste is such that you are unlikely to want to eat any more.

Popular species and varieties: *Arbutus unedo* f. *rubra* AGM has pink flowers and abundant berries. *A.* x *andrachnoides* AGM is a beautiful spreading hybrid with cinnamon-coloured bark; it is hardy and more lime-tolerant.

NAME: *AZALEA* SEE *RHODODENDRON*

NAME: *CALLUNA* (HEATHER)

Origin: North America, north and western Europe to Siberia

Type: Evergreen sub-shrubs and ground-cover plants

USDA Zone: Z4

Preferred pH range: 4.5–6.5

Description: To be accurate, heathers are forms of *Calluna*, whereas forms of the genus *Erica* should be referred to as 'heaths'. Regardless of this bit of naming minutiae, the plants are usually sold and grown together, as they are closely related and by and large enjoy the same growing conditions. They both make excellent ground-cover subjects on an acid soil. Although they flower more prolifically in full sun, they are tolerant of some shade and are therefore suitable to grow under the dappled conditions afforded by certain trees. For example, they associate well with light, deciduous trees such as birch (*Betula*) and rowan (*Sorbus*), both natural choices for an acid soil, and colonize well beneath the high canopy of mature pines. Callunas flower in summer and early autumn. Many varieties have attractive winter and early spring foliage, which can be as much a feature as the flowers. See also *Erica*.

Popular species and varieties: The best forms are cultivars of *Calluna vulgaris*. 'Beoley Gold' AGM has light green summer foliage, flushed with gold and pale cream, and single white flowers that appear from late summer; 'Golden Turret' has beautiful golden yellow foliage and white flowers; 'H.E. Beale' has greyish-green leaves, and double silvery-pink flowers from mid-autumn; 'Mullion' AGM has green foliage and masses of deep pink flowers; 'Sir John Charrington' AGM has yellow foliage that turns reddish in winter, and lilac flowers; and 'White Lawn' AGM has deep green foliage and white flowers. There are near enough a hundred other cultivars available commercially.

ABOVE *Calluna vulgaris* 'H.E. Beale'

ABOVE *Calluna vulgaris* 'Golden Turret'

ABOVE *Camellia* x *williamsii* 'Donation'

NAME: *CAMELLIA*

Origin: Northern India, Himalayas, Japan, northern Indonesia
Type: Evergreen shrubs
USDA Zone: Z8
Preferred pH range: 4.5–6.5
Description: Along with *Rhododendron* (and *Azalea*) and *Pieris*, the *Camellia* is the other flowering woodland shrub you should have in your acid garden. Camellias are exquisite, with flowers in every shade of white, cream, pink or red. They do not perform well in full sun, preferring instead the dappled to light conditions of a woodland glade. But, equally important, these shrubs need to be sheltered from cold winds – this is often the reason for the buds to fall before the flowers open, ruining what

promises to be a healthy crop of spring flowers. The other rule with camellias is that they should not be planted where the buds and flowers receive early morning sun, as the quick thawing after a frost can weaken the flower cells, again making the buds and blooms fall. Late morning and afternoon sun, in small or dappled doses, is fine. The foliage is perhaps the most handsome of the plain evergreens, and the growth habit is usually tidy and compact.

Popular species and varieties: Here are a few recommendations from the many camellia varieties available. For general planting, forms of *Camellia* x *williamsii* are regarded as the best, having a more free-flowering habit and a more graceful nature. The leaves are similar to *C. japonica*, although often narrower.

Excellent cultivars include 'Anticipation' AGM (deep pink), 'Donation' (deep pink, semi-double – the best-known Camellia of all), 'Contribution' (soft rose pink), 'Debbie' (large flowers of clear pink), 'Saint Ewe' AGM (single, cupped blooms and an open, graceful habit) and 'Les Jury' AGM (double, red flowers). Other hybrids worth growing are 'Leonard Messel' AGM (peach pink), 'Inspiration' AGM (rich pink) and 'Cornish Snow' (white, single and small). Cultivars of *C. japonica* are very popular. Usually they have broad, glossy dark green leaves and a strong, upright habit. Look for 'Adolph Audusson' AGM (blood red, semi-double); 'Alba Simplex' (single flowers of pure white); 'Alba Plena' AGM (large double white flowers); 'Elegans' AGM (peach pink); 'Grand Prix' AGM (scarlet); 'Lavinia Maggi' AGM (large double flowers of pale pink or white, with deep pink stripes), and 'Masayoshi' AGM, sometimes known as 'Donckelaeri' (soft red, large and double).

NAME: *CORYLOPSIS* (WINTER HAZEL)

Origin: China
Type: Deciduous shrubs
USDA Zone: Z6
Preferred pH range: 5.5–7.0
Description: Regarded as delightful shrubs, forms of *Corylopsis* are closely related to witch hazel (*Hamamelis*). They are underrated, and should be grown much more often. The flowers are yellow, pendent and delicately scented. You will need an acid soil to grow these plants to perfection.
Popular species and varieties: *C. pauciflora* AGM is the most often seen species, with flowers that are extremely pale, primrose-yellow, and borne in hanging, translucent clusters. They are cowslip-scented. *C. sinensis* var. *sinensis* AGM is a beauty, and so is the cultivar 'Spring Purple', which is larger and has striking purple stems that contrast well with the leaves and pale lemon-yellow flowers.

ABOVE *Corylopsis sinensis* var. *sinensis* AGM

ABOVE *Crinodendron hookerianum* AGM

NAME: *CRINODENDRON HOOKERIANUM* AGM

Origin: Chile
Type: Evergreen shrubs
USDA Zone: Z8
Preferred pH range: 5.5–6.5
Description: This is not the hardiest of plants and is limited to gardens in milder areas. It needs partial shade, so suits an acid woodland garden or a sheltered wall facing the afternoon sun. There are many 'exotic' wall shrubs that do not live up to their descriptions; this is not one of them. Dark, raven-green glossy evergreen foliage, and an upright dense frame, provide the perfect backdrop for the waxy, crimson, lantern-shaped flowers. These hang along the branches on long stalks in late spring.
Popular species and varieties: Normally the straight species if grown, but there is a good cultivar: 'Ada Hoffmann' produces pale pink lanterns on slender foliage. More flower is produced on mature plants.

NAME: *CYTISUS* (BROOM)

Origin: North Africa, western Asia, Europe
Type: Deciduous and evergreen shrubs
USDA Zone: Z5–9
Preferred pH range: 5.0–6.0
Description: The brooms are very colourful shrubs in the pea and bean family. They generally cover themselves with masses of blooms in tones of yellow, cream, orange and sometimes red. There are prostrate forms to bushes of 12ft (4m) or more high. They are excellent for the mixed border, and very successful on hot, dry banks. The lower-growing forms develop into mounds, and these can look particularly good when allowed to flop over a low wall. These are fast-growing but not long-lived shrubs. The leaves (with the exception of *Cytisus battandieri*) are transient, and most of the plant's photosynthesis takes place within the stems and stalks.
Popular species and varieties: There are masses of forms to choose from, and many cultivars have been introduced within the past few years. 'Burkwoodii' AGM flowers in late spring to early summer, with blooms of cerise, and the wings of which are deep crimson edged with yellow. 'Compact Crimson' can be relied upon to make a fine show with its red blooms. 'Killiney Salmon' produces attractive yellow blooms with orange and red markings. My favourite, however, is *C. battandieri* AGM, also known as the pineapple broom, because the golden-yellow flowers do actually smell similar, and are relatively pineapple-shaped. This is a good, deciduous shrub, growing to 12ft (4m) or more.

ABOVE *Cytisus* '**Killiney Salmon**'

NAME: *DABOECIA CANTABRICA* (CONNEMARA HEATH OR ST DABEOC'S HEATH)

Origin: Western Europe

USDA Zone: Z6–8

Preferred pH range: 5.0–6.0

Description: This plant is often thought of as heather, or ling. An evergreen, it is closely related to *Erica* and *Calluna*. The large, round, bell-shaped rose-purple flowers are produced from early summer to late autumn.

Popular species and varieties: All cultivars are forms of *Daboecia cantabrica*. Look for 'Bicolor' AGM (white and pink-purple flowers, some striped, often on the same spike); 'Waley's Red' (deep magenta), *D. cantabrica* subsp. *scotica* 'Jack Drake' AGM (ruby red); *D. cantabrica* subsp. *scotica* 'Silverwells' AGM (white); and subsp. *scotica* 'William Buchanan' AGM (deep purple).

ABOVE *Daboecia cantabrica* subsp. *scotica* '**Silverwells**' AGM

NAME: *ERICA* (HEATH OR HEATHER)

Origin: Africa, Middle East, Europe
Type: Evergreen sub-shrubs
USDA Zone: Z6–10
Preferred pH range: 4.5–6.0
Description: One of the first things a student in gardening college is taught by the lecturers is that plants in the heather family (rhododendrons, azaleas, camellias, *Pieris* and a host of other familiar shrubby plants) generally need an acid soil. Heaths are delightful, tough little plants, and although they are not particularly in fashion at the moment, I think that's a shame. They deserve to be grown more. During the Victorian period and the first part of the twentieth century, heaths and heathers were planted as flowers at the front of beds and borders. Then they went out of vogue. It wasn't until the 1970s that they were put on the map again, and were sold in their tens of millions. Then in the 1990s their popularity started to decline, and today there are many fewer commercial producers of heathers. These plants are hardly ever affected by pests and diseases – that's a tremendous plus point – and there are different types flowering at different times; you can have heathers blooming in your garden near enough all year long. When honeybees are active, the heather flowers are very popular. See also *Calluna* and *Daboecia*.

Popular species and varieties: As for varieties, there are more than a hundred that exist. Most of the winter-flowering types are forms of *Erica carnea*. Four of the best are: 'King George' (dark green leaves accompanied by deep pink flowers from early winter to mid-spring); 'Pink Spangles' AGM (reddish purple flowers appear in late autumn and last all winter); 'Ruby Glow' (pale mauve flowers age to reddish purple, and are carried from mid-winter onwards; and 'Springwood White' AGM (dark green leaves and brilliant white flowers from mid-winter);

ABOVE *Erica* x *darleyensis* 'Furzey' AGM

136

If anyone is uncertain about growing heaths or heathers in their garden, 'Springwood White' AGM is one I would choose to begin with. *E. vagans* 'Mrs D.F. Maxwell' AGM (foliage dark green with bright green tips; flowers deep cerise with dark brown stamens, from early mid summer); 'Valerie Proudley' AGM (foliage bright green at the base of the shoots turning to lemon yellow towards the tips; white flowers from late summer onwards). *E. erigena* is a lime-tolerant winter-flowering heath, although it does much better on a soil between pH5.5–6.5. Look for 'Golden Lady' AGM (golden yellow foliage and white flowers), and 'W.T. Rackliff' AGM (an extremely dense and compact cultivar with dark green foliage and white flowers with brown anthers). Forms of *Erica x darleyensis* are also winter-flowering. These are taller, and often thought of as 'tree heathers'. Look out for 'Darley Dale' (masses of pale pinkish mauve flowers) and 'Furzey' AGM (rose pink). Both of these will also tolerate a marginally lime soil.

NAME: *EUONYMUS* (SPINDLEBERRY OR SPINDLE TREE)

Origin: Asia, Europe, North and Central America, Australia, Madagascar
Type: Evergreen or deciduous shrubs and trees
USDA Zone: Z3–9
Preferred pH range: 5.5–7.0
Description: These may be small trees, or large or small shrubs. The three most frequently seen members of the genus are variegated evergreen forms of *Euonymus fortunei*, widely used for ground cover. However, there are many other species, and the deciduous ones are grown principally for their rich autumn colours and distinctive fruits (which follow the somewhat inconspicuous flowers). The fruit is a capsule that has four or five segments. It ripens to pink or yellow-green, when the segments open to show the seeds. These are white, but have a fleshy, orange covering.
Popular species and varieties: The deciduous forms are mainly forms of *Euonymus europaeus*;

ABOVE *Euonymus* 'Emerald 'n' Gold' AGM

this is found in hedgerows and will make a small tree. The form 'Red Cascade' AGM has some of the finest autumn colour, and some of the finest rosy-red seed capsules. It is a good idea, if you have the room, to grow several of these together, as this will assist in cross-pollination and guarantee a good show of berries. *E. fortunei* 'Emerald 'n' Gold' AGM has green, gold and pink leaves; 'Emerald Gaiety' AGM has green and cream leaves; and 'Silver Queen' has leaves with white edges.

ABOVE *Fuchsia magellanica* var. *gracilis* **AGM**

Popular species and varieties: *Fuchsia magellanica* var. *gracilis* AGM is a very graceful and pretty shrub, with slender, arching stems and numerous small, delicate flowers of scarlet and purple. 'Mrs Popple' AGM has a compact habit, and large flowers of scarlet and violet; 'Riccartonii' AGM is probably the best fuchsia for general planting where a tall shrub can be accommodated. 'Tom Thumb' AGM is a dwarf shrub, with masses of small, freely produced blooms of scarlet and violet. 'Lady Thumb' AGM is similar in habit, with red and white flowers. 'Snowcap' AGM is larger, and has red and white flowers.

ABOVE *Gaultheria forrestii*

NAME: *FUCHSIA* (HARDY FUCHSIA)

Origin: South America, East Africa, Hawaii, New Zealand, Ireland
Type: Deciduous shrubs
USDA Zone: Z6
Preferred pH range: 5.5–6.5
Description: Although hardy fuchsias are called 'hardy' they really only do well in milder locations, and a really severe winter will cause them serious damage. They flower from early summer until late autumn; I regularly have flowers on my plants in early winter when a night frost can give a coating to the last remaining of them.

NAME: *GAULTHERIA*

Origin: North and South America
Type: Evergreen (sometimes dioecious) shrubs
USDA Zone: Z6–10
Preferred pH range: 5.5–6.5
Description: *Gaultheria mucronata* used to be known as *Pernettya mucronata*, and many gardeners and nurserymen still refer to it by this name. It cannot fail to attract attention with its marble-like berries carried on dense thickets of wiry stems. The berries range from white through shades of pink to deep burgundy red. For best effect, plant in groups, with non-berrying male plants to assist pollination and fruit set.
Popular species and varieties: The variety 'Bell's Seedling' AGM is both male and female, with deep green foliage on reddish stems. Large, dark red berries follow the white flowers. *Gaultheria forrestii* is a lovely form but very rarely seen; it has thick and leathery leaves and produces masses of white flowers in spring. Beware, however, as it is slightly tender.

NAME: *GREVILLEA* (SILK OAK)

Origin: Australia
Type: Evergreen shrubs and trees
USDA Zone: Z9
Preferred pH range: 5.5–7.0
Description: Members of the *Protea* family, the grevilleas are exceptionally hardy, despite coming originally from hot climates. They thrive in open sun with good drainage.
Popular species and varieties: The cultivar 'Canberra Gem' AGM is good for coastal gardens and has waxy foliage and clusters of bright pink flowers. 'Robyn Gordon' has fern-like foliage and striking bottlebrush-like flowers. *Grevillea rosmarinifolia* AGM is a lovely, light, sprawling shrub with long, soft shoots and narrow, rosemary-like leaves. Late winter to early summer, curly crimson flowers bloom at the end of the shoots. *G. juniperina* has prickly, narrow foliage; it is a stunning evergreen with greenish-yellow to red flowers from spring to mid-summer.

ABOVE *Grevillea juniperina*

ABOVE *Hamamelis* x *intermedia* 'Vesna'

ABOVE *Hydrangea macrophylla* (Hortensia) 'Altona' AGM

NAME: *HAMAMELIS* (WITCH HAZEL)

Origin: North America, Japan, China
Type: Deciduous shrubs and small trees
USDA Zone: Z5–6
Preferred pH range: 5.5–7.0
Description: The *Hamamelis* genus is not large, but it comprises some remarkable shrubs (even small trees). As well as their strangely delicate flowers produced in the depths of winter, witch hazels contribute some of the best autumn foliage colour in the garden. These are best grown as freestanding specimens in a lawn, rather than as a mere component to a mixed or shrub border. They have a spreading nature, with irregular branch patterns. For this reason you should avoid pruning them if at all possible; these plants should be free spirits!
Popular species and varieties: *Hamamelis* x *intermedia* 'Pallida' AGM is the most popular of the named x *intermedia* clones. Sulphur yellow flowers cover the naked branches in mid-winter. 'Jelena' AGM has red and orange flowers, and superb autumn colour. 'Diane' AGM is truly red. 'Vesna' is a deep golden yellow. *H. mollis* AGM is the Chinese witch hazel. Its large flowers are sweetly fragrant, with broader ribbon-petals than most forms.

NAME: *HYDRANGEA*

Origin: China, Japan, Indonesia, Philippines, North and South America
Type: Woodland shrubs
USDA Zone: Z3–9
Preferred pH range: 4.0–5.0 (blue); 6.0–7.5 (pink)
Description: The woodland garden (that is, any lightly shaded garden) in summer should possess one or two mophead hydrangeas (the

Hortensia group of *Hydrangea macrophylla*). These familiar blue or pink, rounded-headed plants can be hugely dramatic. Some pink varieties are blue on acid soils. On shallow chalk soils the foliage becomes pale, almost yellow; mulching and feeding can remedy this. On alkaline soils, blueing powder can be used to attempt to change the colour to blue, but in reality it is not worth the effort in open ground. White varieties cannot be changed but will often blush pink as their flowers age, especially if growing in full sun. The white or green lacecap group of *H. macrophylla* produces distinctive flowerheads of fertile florets surrounded by a ring of sterile florets. Although not as colourful or as dramatic as the mopheads, these are lighter and prettier, and more satisfactory in mixed plantings.

Popular species and varieties: *Hydrangea macrophylla* (Hortensia) has numerous varieties, and among the best are 'Ami Pasquier' AGM (purple on acid soil, red on a chalky soil), 'Blauer Prinz' (blue on acid, pink on chalk) and 'Altona' AGM (blue on acid, rose-pink on chalk). Of *H. macrophylla* (Lacecap), look for 'Lanarth White' AGM, with flat heads of pink or blue surrounded by large white ray-florets; and 'Mariesii Perfecta' AGM (sometimes sold as 'Blue Wave'), a strong-growing shrub with large heads varying from pink to deep gentian-blue. *H. aspera* Villosa Group AGM is a pink-lilac lacecap type. *H. paniculata* 'Grandiflora' AGM is one of the most breathtaking and showy of large shrubs. It cannot fail to grab attention as it erupts from the back of the border, with its large conical flowerheads resembling huge lilac blossoms. The flowers start to appear pale green in summer, then turn slowly through cream to creamy white with flushes of pink. In shade the cream colour is more pure. The oak-leaved hydrangea (*H. quercifolia* AGM) is of medium size, with bold lobed leaves that resemble those of oak – but are much bigger. They also produce fine autumn colour.

NAME: *KALMIA LATIFOLIA* (CALICO BUSH)

Origin: United States, Cuba
Type: Evergreen shrubs
USDA Zone: Z2–8
Preferred pH range: 4.5–5.0
Description: This is a beautiful, rhododendron-like shrub, with glossy, mid-green foliage. In late spring and early summer it produces clusters of pretty, bright pink flowers. The flower buds look like piped blobs of icing, and even the open, cup-shaped flowers seem to have an icing-sugar quality about them. Many gardeners find that it is a difficult shrub to get started, but it is worth it when established. It is a good idea to stake even small plants after planting; the roots take time to establish.

Popular species and varieties: There are many cultivars available, but few have the charm and pretty disposition of the species. Perhaps the best is 'Ostbo Red', with similar flowers but smaller and darker foliage than the species.

ABOVE *Kalmia latifolia*

ABOVE *Magnolia stellata* 'Rosea'

NAME: *MAGNOLIA*

Origin: Japan, Himalayas, eastern North America to tropical America

Type: Deciduous and evergreen trees and shrubs

USDA Zone: Z4–9

Preferred pH range: 5.0–6.0

Description: Magnolias can be a stunning sight in full bloom during the spring months. Their flowers, almost other-worldly in appearance, seem all the more miraculous when they burst from bare branches before the leaves appear. These are mostly deciduous, although there are evergreen forms (but they are much less dramatic). As for soil, they are tolerant of heavy clay and all prefer acid to neutral, but a few will tolerate reasonably low alkaline levels. Many forms are too large for the average garden, and some of the tree forms can take several years before they reach flowering size. The earliest-flowering types are susceptible to frost and wind damage to the flowers, so choose a sheltered site where possible.

Popular species and varieties: *Magnolia stellata* AGM is arguably the best choice for a small garden. A slow-growing shrub, it forms a compact, broad shrub, eventually reaching 10ft (3m) in height. The winter buds on the bare branches are grey and hairy, opening to white flowers in early spring. They have narrow petals, rounded at the tips, and they are sweetly scented. 'Centennial' is a good cultivar, and seems to be even more floriferous than the species. 'Rosea' bears white, pink-flushed flowers.

M. x *loebneri* is a hybrid of *M. stellata*, with fragrant blooms with long, strap-like petals, opening to flowers that are larger than *stellata*. The best known cultivar is 'Leonard Messell' AGM, with pale lilac-pink flowers. *M. liliiflora* 'Nigra' AGM forms a wide, spreading shrub, and has flowers carried upright on the branches. They are like waxy, deep purple candles, retaining a slender tulip form as they open to reveal a cream-white interior. *M.* x *soulangeana* produces a profusion of large, pointed buds that open to goblet-shaped, creamy white blooms, flushed pink at the base. 'Lennei' AGM has large leaves and flowers, rose-purple outside and creamy white stained pink-purple inside. The hybrid 'Apollo' makes a tree 20ft (6m) high; its features include deep rose-pink buds opening to enormous richly fragrant, rosy red bowl-like flowers up to 10in (25cm) across.

NAME: *PICEA* (SPRUCE)

Origin: Most of the northern hemisphere (except northern Africa)
Type: Evergreen conifers
USDA Zone: Z1–8
Preferred pH range: 4.0–5.0
Description: The spruces include some of the tallest and most beautiful of trees, so a great many are too large for garden use. Fortunately there are plenty that are smaller. They generally have strong main stems, with little side-branching. Most prefer cooler, more moist climates and often do not prosper in hot, dry conditions where they are also more prone to pests and diseases, such as red spider mites.
Popular species and varieties: The White spruce, *Picea glauca* has several excellent forms, the best to my mind being 'Laurin', with a distinctly conical shape and bright green foliage. *P. breweriana* is the most attractive of the common species. The leaves are dark, glossy green on the top side and silvery green on the underside. The familiar and traditional Christmas tree is *P. abies*, but because it readily drops its needles it has mainly been superseded by the similar but longer-lasting Nordmann fir (*Abies nordmanniana*). Neither of these, however, make good garden trees; they are better as forest or 'farmed' trees for the cut Christmas tree industry. *P. orientalis* is an attractive species for its short needles, its maroon male cones and brighter red female cone flowers. 'Aurea' has new foliage which is golden yellow before turning to dark green.

ABOVE *Picea glauca* 'Laurin'

ABOVE *Pieris* 'Forest Flame' AGM

ABOVE *Rhododendron* (Azalea) 'Hinomayo' AGM

NAME: *PIERIS* (FOREST FLAME)

Origin: The Far East, Himalayas, Nepal
Type: Evergreen woodland shrubs
USDA Zone: Z5–7
Preferred pH range: 5.0–6.5
Description: Pieris are at their best in spring, when their displays of white, bell-shaped lily-of-the-valley like blossoms appear, closely followed by the new season's young shoots in fiery reds or delicate pinks and creams. The unfortunate thing is that this new growth is usually produced before the risk of frost has passed, and they are easily scorched by it. The more compact cultivars lend themselves to pots and containers for semi-shade and shelter on the patio.
Popular species and varieties: *Pieris formosa* 'Wakehurst' AGM is strong and vigorous, with short, broad leaves, white flowers and deep, bright red new growth in spring. *P. formosa* var. *forrestii* has superbly vivid red and cream young shoots; *P.* 'Forest Flame' AGM (not to be confused with the common name for the genus) is rather more red; *P. floribunda* is one of the

hardiest, and one of the best for flowers. Two forms of *P. japonica* are certainly worth growing: 'Purity' AGM has very long flower racemes, whilst 'Debutante' AGM is a mound-forming dwarf shrub with short, white flower stems carried in an upright manner.

NAME: *RHODODENDRON*

Origin: Worldwide, mainly the temperate regions of Asia
Type: Deciduous and evergreen small shrubs to medium-sized, spreading trees
USDA Zone: Z5–9
Preferred pH range: 4.5–6.0
Description: The *Rhododendron* genus is enormous. Most are grown for their flower colours in everything from rich vibrant shades to more subtle and pastel colours. They are some of the most spectacular of all flowering plants. Most bloom in spring, although some offer up their colour in mid-winter, whilst others (such as the white-flowering 'Polar Bear') bloom well into summer. A wide variation also is to be had with

ABOVE *Rhododendron arboreum* 'Endsleigh Pink'

the foliage; some forms have leaves barely ¾in (1.5cm) across, whilst others are the size of oval dinner plates. This is a genus of woodland plants, so conditions from dappled to dense shade will suit different types. The genus also includes deciduous and evergreen azaleas, which usually have the strongest-coloured flowers.

Popular species and varieties: The following are all recommended plants for the garden. Among the large-flowered hybrids with pink blooms are 'Augfast Group', 'Loderi Group' and 'Percy Wiseman' AGM (all blush pink), and 'Morgenrot' (deep rose pink, almost red). 'Britannia' and 'Baden-Baden' (both red) are old favourites, and then there is 'Dopey' AGM (bright orange-red). For yellow try 'Julie' (pale lemon), 'Hotei' AGM (deep yellow) and 'Queen Elizabeth II' AGM (greenish yellow). A good white form, 'Helene Schiffner' AGM, has buds that start off mauve, opening to pure white. Similarly the old variety 'Sappho' is excellent, with buds that start off mauve and open to white, but each of the white blooms has a central deep purple blotch. 'Sapphire' is, I believe,

the best of the blues, and even this in some lights looks more like lilac. Of the dwarf rhododendrons look for 'Bengal' (deep red), Blue Tit Group (lavender blue but darkening with age; associate well with heathers) and 'Ginny Gee' AGM (pale pink, fading to white).

The deciduous hybrid azaleas are usually smaller, and prefer being sited in light shade rather than dappled shade. Look for 'Glowing Embers' (orange-red) and 'Gibraltar' AGM (flame orange).

Smaller still are the evergreen hybrid group referred to as Japanese azaleas. They often frequently cover themselves with flower so that you cannot see any leaves. Look for 'Palestrina' AGM (white), 'Mother's Day' AGM (rose red), 'Vuyk's Scarlet' AGM (bright red), 'Hinomayo' AGM (clear pink) and 'Hatsugiri' (magenta-purple). 'Dopey' is one of the best of the reds; large trusses of flowers open in mid-spring, on a dense mound of dark green foliage. *R. arboreum* 'Endsleigh Pink' forms a large shrub, taller than wide; it has small, pale rose flowers.

TREES, SHRUBS AND CLIMBERS PREFERRING SOILS IN THE NEUTRAL RANGE

The following plants thrive in a soil with a pH range that straddles both the higher levels of acidity and the lower levels of alkalinity

Latin name	Common name	pH range
Acacia	Mimosa/Sweet wattle	5.5–7.5
Aronia	–	5.5–7.5
Clematis	–	6.0–8.0*
Clethra	Sweet pepper bush	5.5–7.5
Cornus	Dogwood	5.0–7.5
Cotoneaster	–	6.5–7.5
Crataegus	Hawthorn	6.0–8.0
Enkianthus	–	5.0–7.5
Eucryphia	–	5.5–7.5
Fothergilla	–	5.0–7.5
Globularia	–	5.5–7.5
Hypericum	St John's wort/Rose of Sharon	6.0–8.0
Ilex	Holly	6.0–8.0
Jasminum	Jasmine	6.0–7.5
Juniperus	Juniper	6.5–7.5
Kerria	Jew's mallow	6.0–7.5
Laburnum	Golden rain/Golden	6.0–8.0
Leucothoe	–	6.0–7.5
Liquidambar	Sweet gum	6.0–7.5
Lupinus arboreus	Tree lupin	5.5–7.5
Mahonia	Oregon grape	6.0–7.5
Nyssa	–	5.5–7.5
Prunus laurocerasus	Laurel	5.0–7.5
Rhus	Sumach	5.5–7.5
Rosa	Rose	6.5–8.0

* One of the most commonly held incorrect beliefs about Clematis, known as the 'queen of climbers', is that they must be grown on a chalky soil. This probably arises from Clematis vitalba (known as old man's beard, or traveller's joy); it is a species that occurs naturally on thin, chalky soils, and was traditionally used as a rootstock, onto which were grafted large-flowered hybrids. There is no evidence, however, that clematis in general need chalk to thrive. In fact, they grow perfectly happily on neutral and slightly acid soils, with plenty of moisture available yet being well drained. Sandy soils drain too quickly for clematis and heavy soils are too wet and cold in winter for fine-rooted varieties.

The genus includes some quite beautiful flowering plants, and for almost every garden situation. The normal rule is that the 'top of the plant should be in the sun and the roots should be in the shade', but it is fair to say that many of the popular summer-flowering hybrids offer their best flower-colour when the head of the plant is lightly shaded; intense sunlight can quickly fade and scorch the blooms.

ABOVE *Lupinus arboreus*

ABOVE *Clematis* **'Ruby Glow'**

ABOVE *Cornus canadensis*

VEGETABLES, FRUIT AND HERBS

Earlier in this book I alluded to the fact that there are many types of fruits and vegetables that grow well on – or even prefer – an acid soil. And if your soil is alkaline, then most food crops can also be grown in large tubs and containers with imported acid topsoil.

On the next few pages there is a brief look at the types most suited to acid conditions. For more information on growing fruits and vegetables it is best to consult a more detailed book on the subject (such as *Success with Organic Fruit* and/or *Success with Organic Vegetables*, companion volumes to this book, and also published by GMC Publications).

In this section we lead with the common name of the fruit, vegetable or herb, followed by the botanical Latin in brackets. This is because all gardeners refer to these plants by their common names and it is both clumsy and unnecessary to list them in a less appealing way.

NAME: APPLE (*MALUS DOMESTICA*)

Preferred pH range: 5.5–6.5

Description: There are hundreds of varieties of apples. Of the dessert type, two of the best include: 'Fiesta' AGM (flushed, bright red skin and suitable for cold areas) and 'Greensleeves' AGM (hardy, reliable with crispy green-yellow fruits). For the 'cooker' type, consider 'Arthur Turner' AGM (large, hardy apple for mid-autumn) and 'Howgate Wonder' (large, pale green fruits that turn yellow with brown-red markings).

LEFT **Apple 'Fiesta' AGM**

NAME: BLACKBERRY (*RUBUS FRUTICOSUS*)

Preferred pH range: 5.0–6.0

Description: These cultivated forms of the wild bramble produce vast quantities of fruit over a long season, starting in late summer; sadly the more amenable, thornless varieties are not generally as vigorous. The fruits need lots of watering in dry weather otherwise fruiting suffers. 'Oregon Thornless' has a good flavour and is easy to train. 'Bedford Giant' is an early variety with very long canes and a good flavour.

LEFT **Blackberry 'Oregon Thornless'**

NAME: BLUEBERRY (*VACCINIUM* spp.)

Preferred pH range: 4.5–6.0

Description: There are 'highbush' and 'lowbush' blueberries; the former tolerate some shade (but prefer full sun), whilst the latter need sun. They also like a cool, moist climate. The purple-black fruits, covered in a grey 'bloom', are delicious in cooked desserts, but need to be really ripe to be enjoyed raw. 'Berkeley' is the best-known variety; it is a mid-season crop. 'Bluecrop' is an upright-growing early cropper, and 'Jersey' is a compact late-season variety.

LEFT **Blueberry 'Berkeley'**

NAME: CARROT (*DAUCUS CAROTA*)

Preferred pH range: 5.5–6.5

Description: Carrots vary in length, depending on the variety grown. The soil should be acid, well-drained, stone-free (otherwise the roots 'fork') and it should not have been manured during the previous year. 'Chantenay' is an early maincrop variety; 'Resistafly F1' has long roots and enjoys good resistance to the carrot fly pest; and 'Artemis F1' is winter hardy and able to hold in the ground over winter until early spring.

LEFT **Carrot 'Artemis F1'**

NAME: CHICORY (*CICHORIUM INTYBUS*)

Preferred pH range: 5.0–6.5

Description: The slightly bitter, young, blanched leaves of chicory are delicious in salads. Red- and green-leaved varieties include 'Witloof' (a good 'forcing' variety, with dense yellow-green heads); 'Normato' (a modern forcing variety); 'Sugar Loaf', also known as 'Pain de Sucre' (the traditional non-forcing variety); 'Crystal Head', 'Snowflake' and 'Winter Fare' (hardy non-forcing varieties); and 'Rossa De Verona' (a red-leaved chicory). It can be grown outdoors over winter.

LEFT **Chicory 'Sugar Loaf'**

NAME: FIG (*FICUS CARICA*)

Preferred pH range: 5.0–7.0

Description: The fruits, which grow over two seasons, are wonderfully sweet and exotic but plants are sometimes grown just for the architectural appearance of their leaves. They can be vigorous growers, so contain their roots if the garden is small. The most popular varieties include: 'Brunswick' (very sweet when ripe); 'Brown Turkey' AGM (reddish fruits and a heavy cropper); and 'White Marseilles' (with a whitish, almost transparent flesh).

LEFT **Fig 'Brunswick'**

NAME: FLORENCE FENNEL (*FOENICULUM VULGARE* VAR. *DULCE*)

Preferred pH range: 5.0–7.0

Description: Grown for its aniseed-flavoured swollen leaf bases, or 'bulbs'; the ferny foliage can also be used as meal decoration or garnish. 'Romanesco', a 'sweet Florence' type, produces large white bulbs; 'Finale' is smaller, but the bulbs tend to be more uniform in growth and this variety also has good resistance to bolting (premature running to seed). Not to be confused with the chalk soil-loving straight species – the herb fennel (*Foeniculum vulgare*) – the leaves of which are used to flavour fish and poultry dishes.

LEFT **Florence fennel**

NAME: GOOSEBERRY (*RIBES UVA-CRISPA*)

Preferred pH range: 5.0–6.5

Description: Although not universally popular, gooseberries can give a very good return for the amount of space and effort devoted to growing them. Apart from the usual green varieties there are reds, whites and yellows. Look for: 'Lord Derby' (large, round dark fruits, smooth skin, good flavour); 'Leveller' AGM (large, oval, yellow-green, good cropper, excellent flavour); and 'Invicta' AGM (large red fruits, late-ripening, very good flavour).

LEFT **Gooseberry 'Lord Derby'**

NAME: MELON (*CUCUMIS MELO*)

Preferred pH range: 5.5–6.5

Description: In cooler temperate climates it is often necessary to grow melons in greenhouses or frames. Cantaloupes have a rough, grooved or greyish skin and green or orange flesh; 'Ogen' has orange-yellow skin, pale green flesh, good flavour; 'Sweetheart' has medium-sized fruits with a salmon pink flesh, excellent flavour. Musk melons are smaller, with fine 'netting' on smooth skins, and a musky flavour; 'Ringleader' has large, oval, orange-yellow fruits with green flesh, very good flavour; and 'Antalya', is a round, medium-sized fruit with light-green, sweet and aromatic flesh.

LEFT **Melon 'Antalya'**

NAME: PARSLEY (*PETROSELINUM CRISPUM*)

Preferred pH range: 5.0–7.0

Description: The bright green, feathery foliage of parsley has a strong, aromatic flavour and is best used in hot dishes and as an accompaniment to fish. It does not dry well, but can be frozen. The usual form grown is the species (referred to as moss-curled parsley); the cultivar 'Bravour' AGM has a particularly fine habit and leaves of a deeper green. Alternatives include the French or Italian parsley (*P. crispum* var. *neapolitanum*) which has flat leaves and a similar flavour, and Hamburg parsley (*P. crispum* var. *tuberosum*), grown for its thick, edible roots.

LEFT **Parsley 'Bravour' AGM**

NAME: POTATO

Preferred pH range: 4.5–6.0

Description: Most potato varieties have white or pinkish-red skin and white flesh, but there are also yellow, pink or blue-fleshed varieties. Tubers for growing are sold as 'first early' varieties (planted in early spring), 'second early' (planted in mid-spring) and 'maincrop' (planted in late spring). Lifting can take place from early summer onwards. There are literally hundreds of varieties to choose from, so it is best to consult a specialist's catalogue.

LEFT **'First early' potatoes are the first potatoes of the year to be lifted, in early summer.**

NAME: RASPBERRY (*RUBUS IDAEUS*)

Preferred pH range: 5.0–6.5

Description: These are good croppers for cool climates, but do not seem to do as well in the warmer Mediterranean (or hotter) regions. There are red fruits and yellow fruits, and there are summer croppers and autumn croppers. Apart from colour and timing, there is little to distinguish between flavours, however. Look for: 'Malling Jewel' AGM, 'Polka' and 'Glen Rosa' (large, juicy, red fruits); and 'Aureus' and 'Fallgold' (sweet and mild-flavoured, golden yellow fruits).

LEFT **Raspberry 'Polka'**

NAME: ROSEMARY (*ROSMARINUS OFFICINALIS*)

Preferred pH range: 5.0–6.0

Description: This woody herb has long, thin leaves that are green on top and grey-white underneath. When you brush the plant or scrunch the leaves, there is a spicy, peppery aroma. Harvest fresh sprigs to flavour roasts, stews, stuffings and sauces. Pale-blue flowers appear in spring and summer. 'Miss Jessop's Upright' AGM is the nicest-looking cultivar (and makes a good hedging plant, too). *R. officinalis* var. *albiflorus* has white flowers

LEFT **Rosemary 'Miss Jessop's Upright' AGM**

VEGETABLES, FRUIT AND HERBS PREFERRING SOILS IN THE NEUTRAL RANGE

The following plants thrive in a soil with a pH range that straddles both the higher levels of acidity and the lower levels of alkalinity:

VEGETABLES

Name	pH range
Broccoli	6.0–7.5
Celery	6.0–7.5
Courgettes	5.5–7.5
Lettuce	6.0 7.5
Onion	6.0–7.5
Pepper	5.5–7.5
Radish	6.0–7.5
Rhubarb	5.5–7.5
Shallot	5.5 7.5
Swede	5.5–7.5
Turnip	5.5–7.5

FRUIT

Name	pH range
Apricot	6.0–7.5
Grapevine	6.0–7.5
Hazelnut	6.0–7.5
Lemon	6.0–7.5
Red currant	5.5–7.5

HERBS

Name	pH range
Chives	6.0–7.5
Horseradish	6.0–7.5
Sage	6.0–7.5
Thyme	5.5–7.5

HOUSE AND CONSERVATORY PLANTS

The acidity level of soils is important to all soil-growing plants (for some plants are epiphytic – having no or few roots, and so grow naturally on tree branches). Where house or indoor plants in pots are concerned, the pH levels are still relevant. Some of our most popular indoor plants need high acidity (or high alkalinity) if they are to thrive.

Over the next four pages we take a quick look at the types most suited to acid conditions. For more detail on growing houseplants it is best to consult a specialist book on the subject.

NAME: *AECHMEA* (URN PLANT)

Preferred pH range: 5.0–5.5

Description: The natural home of this plant is near the floor of the rainforest, where water from the tree canopy drips on to the tough, leathery, strap-shaped leaves. The most commonly grown form is *Aechmea fasciata* AGM, which has green leaves covered with a silvery-white 'down'. In mature plants a central, pink flower stalk emerges from the centre of the leaves. *A. fasciata* 'Purpurea' has maroon leaves and silver marking.

LEFT *Aechmea fasciata* AGM

NAME: *ABUTILON* (FLOWERING MAPLE)

Preferred pH range: 5.5–6.5

Description: This is a tender plant, related to the mallow family. All species in this large genus are grown for their bell-shaped drooping flowers and maple-like leaves on long stalks. *Abutilon* x *hybridum* is the name given to a group of hybrids that are generally available from garden centres. Look for: 'Savitzii' (with the palest of green leaves); 'Cannington Red' (golden yellow leaves and rose-red blooms) and 'Kentish Belle' (with vibrant orange flowers).

LEFT **Abutilon hybrid**

NAME: *AGAVE* (CENTURY PLANT)

Preferred pH range: 5.0–6.5

Description: This succulent plant is grown for its 'architectural' appeal, and is referred to as the 'century plant' because of the mistaken belief that flowers appear only once every 100 years. In reality they will flower when about ten years old in the wild, but as a pot plant this is unlikely. *Agave americana* AGM has green leaves, but much more attractive, and much more widely available is *A. americana* 'Variegata' AGM, with creamy-yellow margins to the thick, spiny-edged leaves.

LEFT *Agave americana* 'Variegata' AGM

NAME: *ANTHURIUM* (FLAMINGO FLOWER)

Preferred pH range: 5.0–6.0

Description: A spectacularly colourful pot plant from spring through to mid-autumn. The arum-like flowers comprise a large, waxy, usually scarlet, palette-shaped spathe from which a narrow spadix emerges. There are a number of white, cream and pink forms too. Look for *Anthurium andreanum* AGM (which has some of the largest flowers in the genus); and *A. scherzerianum* 'Rothschildianum' (red spathe and spotted white and yellow spadix).

LEFT *Anthurium andreanum* AGM

NAME: *CODIAEUM* (CROTON)

Preferred pH range: 5.0–6.0

Description: One of the most colourful of foliage houseplants, the croton is also known as Joseph's coat, and it is not difficult to see why. The tough, leathery leaves are largely yellow-and-green mottled or veined, with rosy pink, red, orange, brown or purple markings. *Codiaeum variegatum* var. *pictum* 'Excellent' has the largest leaves; 'Aucubifolium' has green, laurel-like leaves spotted with yellow.

LEFT *Codiaeum variegatum* var. *pictum* 'Excellent'

NAME: CACTI

Preferred pH range: 4.5–6.0

Description: Cacti are succulent plants with spines. Being succulents, they store water very efficiently, so are well adapted to dry conditions. They usually thrive on neglect, and suffer more from overwatering. They are happy in the brightest of windows, where many other pot plants would suffer in the intense light. It is impossible to select just a few from the thousands of species and cultivars available; it is far better to consult a specialist book such as *Success with Cacti and Other Succulents*, also from GMC Publications.

LEFT **Cactus collection on display.**

NAME: *DIONAEA MUSCIPULA* (VENUS FLY TRAP)

Preferred pH range: 4.0–5.0

Description: The archetypal meat-eating or carnivorous plant, with clam-like leaf structures that clasp shut over unsuspecting flies. As carnivorous plants come from areas where their roots cannot obtain sufficient nutrients from the soil (usually highly acidic marshes and bogs), they have developed a way of absorbing nutrients from animals, living or dead. They are really grown by amateurs as curios, for they can hardly be described as attractive. They require some of the most acidic soils of any plant in this book.

LEFT *Dionaea muscipula*

NAME: *FICUS* (RUBBER PLANTS)

Preferred pH range: 5.0–6.0

Description: There are masses of species within the *Ficus* genus. Most familiar are the Indian rubber plant (*Ficus elastica*), as well as the weeping fig (*F. benjamina*), the creeping fig (*F. pumila*) and the fiddle-leaf fig (*F. lyrata*). There are more attractive variegated forms of *F. elastica* and *F. benjamina*. As well as acidic compost, all *Ficus* demand a humid atmosphere; otherwise leaves can drop at an alarming rate.

LEFT *Ficus elastica* 'Variegata'

NAME: *PHILODENDRON*

Preferred pH range: 5.0–6.0

Description: These have waxy leaves that are essentially green. The most popular type is the heartleaf philodendron (*Philodendron scandens*), but there is also the blushing philodendron (*P. erubescens*), so-called because of the reddish margins to its leaves. The largest-leaved form is the tree philodendron (*P. bipinnatifidum*), with dark glossy green leaves which, when mature, have deep indentations.

LEFT *Philodendron bipinnatifidum*

NAME: *PEPEROMIA*

Preferred pH range: 5.0–6.0

Description: Small plants that are ideal as sunless windowsill plants, peperomias can last for many years. The emerald ripple (*Peperomia caperata*) has deeply veined heart-shaped green leaves and tall poker-like flower spikes. The desert privet (*P. obtusifolia*) meanwhile has smooth, waxy oval leaves; it also has a number of variegated forms. *P. scandens* is the cupid peperomia, and has much smaller leaves on creeping stems.

LEFT *Peperomia obtusifolia* 'Variegata'

NAME: *STRELITZIA REGINAE* AGM (BIRD OF PARADISE)

Preferred pH range: 6.0–6.5

Description: Also known as the crane flower, this spectacular plant has flowers that look like the head of the exotic crested crane. Bright orange-and-blue-petalled flowers emerge from green bracts to form a colourful 'crest'. Flowers don't usually appear on plants younger than five or six years. Each flower lasts about a week, but each stalk produces several that open in succession. Only the species is generally available.

LEFT *Strelitzia reginae* AGM

NAME: *SYNGONIUM* (ARROWHEAD PLANT)

Preferred pH range: 5.0–6.0

Description: This plant is grown for its climbing ability and its attractive foliage. The leaves start off more or less heart-shaped when young, gradually becoming arrowhead-shaped, then lobed and divided into segments as the plant matures. The varieties have different patterns of pale green, white or cream markings on the leaves. 'Butterfly' has deep green leaves with lighter veins; 'Pixie' is compact and small-leave

LEFT *Syngonium* 'Butterfly'

NAME: *TOLMEIA MENZIESII* (PIGGYBACK PLANT)

Preferred pH range: 5.0 6.0

Description: The main feature of this plant is that young plantlets form at the base of the older leaves, giving the plant its common name. It forms a mound of hairy, bright green, roughly heart-shaped leaves, which are lobed and have toothed margins. Tubular, greenish, rather insignificant flowers occasionally appear in summer. A yellow-splashed form, 'Variegata', bears both variegated and plain leaves and is often grown. It may also be sold under the name 'Taff's Gold'.

LEFT *Tolmeia menziesii*

HOUSE AND CONSERVATORY PLANTS PREFERRING SOILS IN THE NEUTRAL RANGE

The following plants thrive in a soil with a pH range that straddles both the higher levels of acidity and the lower levels of alkalinity:

Latin name	Preferred pH
Aglaonema	5.0–7.5
Aphelandra	5.0–7.5
Aspidistra	4.0–7.5
Begonia	5.5–7.5
Calathea	5.0–7.5
Calceolaria	6.0–7.5
Capsicum	5.0–7.5
Cissus	5.0–7.5
Clivia	5.5–7.5
Crassula	5.0–7.5
Epipremnum	5.0–6.0
Fittonia	5.5–7.5
Gardenia	5.0–7.5
Gynura	5.5–7.5
Helxine	5.0–7.5
Hoya	5.0–7.5
Iresine	5.5–7.5
Lantana	5.5–7.5
Maranta	5.0–7.5
Monstera	5.0–7.5
Sansevieria	4.5–7.0
Schlumbergera	5.0–6.5
Succulents	5.0–6.5
Tradescantia	5.0–6.0
Zebrina	5.0–6.0

Glossary

Acid
With a pH value below 7; acid soil is deficient in lime and basic minerals.

Alkaline
With a pH value above 7.

Annual
Plant grown from seed that germinates, flowers, sets seed and dies in one growing year.

Bare-root
Plants sold with their roots bare of soil (i.e. not in a pot or container).

Biennial
A plant that grows from seed and completes its life cycle within two years.

Cultivar
A cultivated plant clearly distinguished by one or more characteristics and which retains these characteristics when propagated; a contraction of 'cultivated variety', and often abbreviated to 'cv.' in plant naming.

Deciduous
Plant that loses its leaves at the end of every growing year, and which renews them at the start of the next.

Double
Referred to in flower terms as a bloom with several layers of petals; usually there would be a minimum of 20 petals. 'Very double' flowers have more than 40 petals.

Genus (pl. Genera)
A category in plant naming, comprising a group of related species.

Heeling in
Laying plants in the soil, with the roots covered, as a temporary measure until full planting can take place.

Humus
Organic matter (derived from plant or animal waste) that has been broken down by bacteria in the soil, resulting in a black, crumbly substance from which plants can easily extract nutrients.

Hybrid
The offspring of genetically different parents, usually produced in cultivation, but occasionally arising in the wild.

Lime
Compounds of calcium. This can be used to 'sweeten' an acidic soil, to make it suitable for growing a wider range of plants.

Mulch
Layer of material applied to the soil surface, to conserve moisture, improve its structure, protect roots from frost and suppress weeds.

Peat
Partially decayed organic matter. Usually acid, it is used for adding to composts and mulches. For environmental reasons, it is better to use peat substitutes such as coconut fibre or bark.

Perennial
Plant that lives for at least three seasons.

Photosynthesis
The process of food manufacture in plants, whereby chlorophyll in leaves traps the sun's energy, combines it with carbon dioxide from the air and hydrogen in water and creates carbohydrates.

pH scale
A scale measured from 1–14 that indicates the alkalinity or acidity of soil. pH 7 is neutral; pH 1–7 is acid; pH 7–14 is alkaline.

Ray- floret
The 'petals' of the flowers of some members of the daisy family.

Rhizome

A branched underground stem that bears roots and shoots.

Rootstock

A plant used to provide the root system for a grafted plant.

Scorch

Leaves turning brown and dry as a result of bright sunlight or hot weather (also cold winds and chemical spray damage).

Sideshoot

A stem that arises from the side of a main shoot or stem.

Single

In flower terms, a single layer of petals opening out into a fairly flat shape, comprising no more than five petals.

Species

A category in plant naming, the rank below genus, containing related, individual plants.

Sub-shrub

A plant that produces some woody mature growth, but the soft growth of which will die down in winter.

Sucker

Generally a shoot that arises from below ground, emanating from a plant's roots, but also refers to any shoot on a grafted plant that originates from below the graft union.

Topsoil

The fertile, upper-most layer of soil.

Transpiration

Part of the natural process of photosynthesis whereby plants lose water through their leaves into the atmosphere. Should the rate of transpiration exceed the rate of water intake via the roots, the plant will dehydrate and start to wilt.

Variety

Botanically, a naturally occurring variant of a wild species; usually shorted to 'var.' when used in plant naming.

About the author

Graham Clarke lives with his wife and two daughters in Dorest, on England's south coast. Here the air is clear, with a mild climate that is far drier than most other parts of the UK.

Graham was born into gardening – literally. His father was in charge of the world-famous Regent's Park in London and at the time of Graham's birth the family lived in a lodge within the gardens there. During his formative years Graham was surrounded by quality horticulture, so it was little surprise when he chose this as his career.

He went to study with England's Royal Horticultural Society at Wisley Gardens, and after that worked as a gardener at Buckingham Palace in London. This very private garden is seen by Her Majesty the Queen on most of the days she is in residence.

For more than 25 years Graham has been a gardening writer and journalist. He has written a dozen books, and countless articles for most of the major UK gardening magazines. At various times he was editor of *Amateur Gardening* (the UK's leading weekly magazine for amateurs) and *Horticulture Week* (the UK's leading weekly magazine for professionals).

Over the years he has gardened on a wide range of soils, and is on record as saying that his acid-soil gardens have been the most rewarding.

Index

Pages highlighted in **bold** indicate photographs of plants.

GMC Publications Ltd, 166 High Street, Lewes, East Sussex BN7 1XU, United Kingdom
Tel: 01273 488005 Fax: 01273 402866
www.gmcbooks.com

Contact us for a complete catalogue, or visit our website.